796.35
MO

Morelli, Jack
Heroes of the Negro
Leagues

Heroes of the Negro Leagues

HEROES
of the
NEGRO LEAGUES

· ·

Written by **JACK MORELLI**
Illustrated by **MARK CHIARELLO**

Introduction by
MONTE IRVIN

Abrams, New York

THE ROSTER

INTRODUCTION

by Monte Irvin

Some of the best players of all time showcased their greatness on the proving grounds of the ballparks of the Negro Leagues. I consider myself fortunate to have been an eyewitness to this part of baseball history as a player with the Newark Eagles in the Negro National League. During the years that I was with the Eagles, I had the privilege of playing with and against many players who are now in the Baseball Hall of Fame.

Let me start with my teammates. Our shortstop, Willie Wells, was a great fielder, could run, and was a good hitter. He was part of the Eagles' "million dollar" infield, along with third baseman Ray Dandridge. I've seen a lot of third basemen but I've never seen anybody who got the ball to first base faster than Dandridge. He came underhanded with his throws and—no matter if the ball was hit hard or soft—he would get the runner by a step. Mule Suttles was known mostly for his hitting. He was one of the best curveball hitters I ever saw and could hit a ball as far as anybody. Leon Day was cat-quick and a great pitcher. In addition to his fastball, he had a quick curve and good control. He was lionhearted and would always throw as hard as he could for as long as he could.

In 1946, when we won the Negro World Series, Biz Mackey was our manager. In his prime, Biz had been the top catcher in the league before Josh Gibson came along. Dick Lundy managed the Eagles a few years earlier. His nickname was "King Richard" because in his prime, he was king of the shortstops. Lundy should be in the Hall of Fame.

The best team in our league was the Homestead Grays, who featured the power tandem of Josh Gibson and Buck Leonard. Josh was a natural-born player. He had a great physique with upper body strength that generated tremendous bat speed. His power was incredible. He was fearless at the plate and was a great clutch hitter. Right behind him was Buck Leonard. Buck didn't hit balls as far as Josh, but he hit home runs, too. He had one of the quickest bats I've ever seen, and was a dead-pull hitter who feasted on fastballs.

Another player that I want to mention is the Elites' Bill Wright. Bill was the fastest big man I ever saw. He could run like a deer and he was a master of the drag bunt. Without question he should be elected to the Hall of Fame.

I saw Oscar Charleston when he was playing first base for the Pittsburgh Crawfords. He was outstanding—a great hitter. In his prime he had played centerfield, and he was the Willie Mays of that era. But I'll say this: I played with Willie and nobody in the world ever played centerfield better than Willie Mays. Charleston was mean, aggressive, and strong. He and Josh Gibson would get into a debate in the dugout about who was strongest, and they would grab each other and wrestle like two bull elephants. Most times it ended in a tie.

Over in the Negro American League there were also many talented players. Best known, of course, is Satchel Paige. He was a natural: fearless, smart, and confident. He thought he could get anybody out. When I first saw him, he didn't have a curveball. He threw fastballs in and out, up and down.

Satchel's teammates on the Kansas City Monarchs included Hilton Smith, Willard Brown, and Buck O'Neil. Hilton had a great curveball that was almost unhittable. Willard was their premier slugger—he killed a high fastball—and he could run. When he went up to the St. Louis Browns, they should have sent him down to the minors for a couple of months to learn the major league way of doing things.

Buck was a smooth-fielding first baseman and a pretty good hitter. I think he belongs in the Hall of Fame because of his overall contributions to baseball.

I played against Martin Dihigo in Mexico in 1942. Martin could do everything. He played every position except catcher. As a pitcher, he was the Satchel Paige of Latin America. He was tall, with a regal-like manner about him.

It is always gratifying to see players from the Negro Leagues get their just recognition as outstanding baseball players and also for their contributions to the game of baseball. I tip my hat to the players who are included in this book, as representatives of all the players who played in the Negro Leagues.

Josh Gibson

BORN: DECEMBER 21, 1911, BUENA VISTA, GEORGIA
DIED: JANUARY 20, 1947
BATS: RIGHT / THROWS: RIGHT

Elected to the Baseball Hall of Fame in 1972

Joshua Gibson began his career in 1929 as a catcher on the Homestead Grays. The jovial, Georgia-born right-hander was a fine backstop with a mighty arm. He possessed surprising speed and a tremendous work ethic. But it was his mammoth slugging power that earned him the name "The Black Babe Ruth."

Pitchers shuddered when the 6'1", 215-pound Gibson dug in, rolled up his left sleeve, and thumped home plate. Josh hit more home runs than anyone in the Negro Leagues, driving one out every dozen times up, and he smashed them out of sight. During a Negro League Day at Yankee Stadium, Gibson blasted a rocket off Slim Jones that cleared the third tier and made the street—something no other man has ever done. Over 20,000 fans sat awestruck as officials walked off a 550-foot moonshot he launched in St. Louis. Gibson hit for average, too. His lifetime .391 is the Negro Leagues' top, and he batted .412 against major leaguers. He was the mighty offensive engine that powered the Homestead Grays and Pittsburgh Crawfords to their numerous Negro League titles. Josh played year-round from 1933 to 1945, wintering in Puerto Rico (.480), Cuba (.353), and Mexico (.373). In nine All-Star appearances, Gibson hit .483. The great Hall of Fame pitcher Walter Johnson estimated his Major League value at two-hundred thousand dollars. The salary he received from the Grays never exceeded six-thousand dollars per year.

During the 1943 season, Josh suffered headaches, dizziness, and blackouts. His behavior became erratic, and then even his legendary physical abilities waned. The diagnosis was a possible brain tumor. Refusing a risky operation, the thirty-three-year-old Gibson battled back in 1944, hitting .338 to lead the league. In 1945, he led again with .393 and, as usual, was home run king both years. But things turned worse in 1946, and for the first time in fourteen years Josh did not play winter ball.

On the night of January 20, 1947, two months before Jackie Robinson made it to the Majors, Josh Gibson, possibly the greatest hitter in baseball history, lay down to sleep and never awoke.

JOSH GIBSON

William "Judy" Johnson

BORN: OCTOBER 26, 1899, SNOW HILL, MARYLAND
DIED: JUNE 15, 1989
BATS: RIGHT / THROWS: RIGHT

Elected to the Baseball Hall of Fame in 1975

Judy Johnson, many old timers insist, was the best third baseman ever—and when the Hall of Fame began inducting men from the Negro Leagues, Judy was the first they picked from that position. He had good range and a tremendous arm, but his greatest asset was his mind. Judy knew baseball.

Born October 26, 1899, in Maryland, the 5'11", 155-pound infielder was baseball's version of the decoding machine. After only an inning or two of watching an opposing manager's hand signals, Johnson would decipher them and pass the information on to his teammates. In his many years with the Homestead Grays, Johnson worked out a sly code of his own with catcher Josh Gibson. Judy would swipe the base-stealing signs coming in from the enemy dugout to their base runner, and would in turn whistle a coded message to Gibson, tipping him off to when and where the runner would be going. Countless players were thrown out before they got anywhere *near* their intended base.

In the field, Johnson's reflexes were enhanced by his ability to judge, from the type of pitch, to where and how hard the ball was likely to be hit. At the plate, he was a contact hitter with a .287 average in a fifteen-year career that spanned 1921 to 1936. His best mark was .416 in 1929. Johnson went to the play-offs six times and the Negro League World Series in 1921, 1924, and 1925. In the 1924 series, playing for Hilldale against Kansas City, he led both teams with an average of .364, including six doubles, a triple, and a homer. When the color line was finally broken, Johnson's playing days were well behind him, but he still had that great baseball mind. He remained in baseball, and was a scout for the Phillies until 1974.

JUDY JOHNSON

John "Buck" O'Neil

BORN: NOVEMBER 13, 1911, CARRABELLE, FLORIDA
DIED: OCTOBER 6, 2006
BATS: RIGHT / THROWS: RIGHT

A soft-spoken champion of the players from baseball's shadow realm, no single person did more to ensure that the legacy of the men of the Negro Leagues was not lost than the graceful, dignified gentleman known as "Buck" O'Neil.

Buck began his career with the Miami Giants in 1934 after graduating from Edward Waters College in Jacksonville. The right-handed Floridian first baseman jumped from team to team for a few years, upping his pay with each move. Then in 1939 he found a lasting home with the Kansas City Monarchs, where he stayed as a player and a manager for the next fifteen years. When the Negro American and National Leagues met in their first World Series in 1942, Buck hit .353 and supplied rock-solid defense as the Kansas City squad swept the Homestead Grays. He left baseball that year to serve in WWII with the famed Fighting Seabees of the navy. Upon his return in 1946, Buck took up where he'd left off by again hitting .353, but this time over the entire season, to win a batting title. By 1948 he was respected as one of the sharpest minds in the game, and took over the reins as the Monarchs' manager. As their skipper he collected five pennants, as well as being elected to manage four consecutive All-Star Games, before his retirement in 1955.

Buck was an asset far too great to be allowed to leave baseball. The Chicago Cubs signed him in 1962 as the first black coach in the Majors. He was also their scout, and was personally responsible for the acquisition of Ernie Banks and Lou Brock. Yet Buck didn't forget his compatriots of old. Determined to keep their memory alive, he helped establish the Negro Leagues Museum in Kansas City, and was chairman of the board. He also served on the Veteran's Committee in Cooperstown, and oversaw the induction of many Negro League players into the National Baseball Hall of Fame.

It was impossible to hear him sing his soft, soulful rendition of "Take Me Out to the Ballgame" without feeling a lump in your throat.

BUCK O'NEIL

Willie Foster

BORN: JUNE 12, 1904, CALVERT, TEXAS
DIED: SEPTEMBER 16, 1978
BATS: BOTH / THROWS: LEFT

Elected to the Baseball Hall of Fame in 1996

Andrew "Rube" Foster was a shrewd baseball genius who would never allow nepotism to enter into a decision concerning the roster of his Chicago American Giants. In fact, he tried to steer his younger brother William *away* from the game. But when Bill began showing the ability that would make him one of the greatest left-handers in the Negro Leagues, Rube told him, "If you're gonna play, you don't play for *anybody* but *me*."

In 1926, Willie won the first twenty-six games he pitched for the American Giants and led them to the World Series against the Bacharachs. There, Foster threw three complete games, winning two, one by a score of 1-0. He also relieved in a fourth game, as the Giants won the series 5-3. 1927 saw the Giants take the series again, as Bill went 2-0 in his championship starts. When the East-West All-Star Game was inaugurated in 1933, Foster was chosen as starting pitcher for the West. He went the distance and got the win over an East team that boasted a "Murderer's Row" line-up of Cool Papa Bell, Oscar Charleston, Jud Wilson, and Josh Gibson. The 6'2", 205-pound strikeout artist was especially hard for batters to figure out because he delivered all of his offerings with the same throwing motion. If you were looking for a clue from Foster as to what might be coming, you were just not going to get it.

Willie Foster had a career-long rivalry with Satchel Paige and, while we may never know who holds the head-to-head win-loss edge, we can be sure it's close. What we do know is that on one day, Foster pitched *both* games of a doubleheader in the hot sun, the second start being against Paige, and he emerged with two complete game victories.

WILLIE FOSTER

John Henry "Pop" Lloyd

BORN: APRIL 25, 1884, PALATKA, FLORIDA
DIED: MARCH 19, 1965
BATS: LEFT / THROWS: RIGHT

Elected to the Baseball Hall of Fame in 1977

Pop Lloyd was called "The Black Honus Wagner." Intrigued by this comparison, the "Flying Dutchman" made it a point to see Pop play. At game's end, Wagner stood up and said, "I am honored that they would name such a great player after me." The 6'1" mild-mannered gentleman from Florida was perhaps the finest shortstop in baseball, black or white. At bat, he was a tremendous line-drive hitter with a high average.

Playing winter ball for the Havana Reds in 1910, Pop heard the Detroit Tigers were coming down for exhibition games and bringing Ty Cobb, a vicious base stealer famous for using his spikes to intentionally tear up opponents' legs. In preparation, Lloyd put iron shin guards under his leggings to deflect Cobb's daggers. Cobb went 0-3 in his attempts on second, as Pop used the shin guards to hook Ty away from the bag as he slapped on the tag. The Cubans adored Lloyd, nicknaming him "Cuchara" (Shovel), for the way his big hands scooped up grounders.

Pop Lloyd's lifetime batting average was .339 against black pitching and .327 against white major leaguers in a twenty-four-year career spanning 1908 to 1931. In 1928, at age forty-four, Pop played in thirty-seven games, hit .564 to lead the league, and led in homers (eleven) and stolen bases (ten). After officially retiring in 1931, he played semipro ball with the Atlantic City Johnson Stars, jokingly vowing not to give up the game "until a lefty strikes me out." He finally hung up his glove in 1942 at age fifty-eight and began to pass his knowledge on to the youth of the community, becoming the commissioner of the Little League. In 1949, Atlantic City honored Pop by naming its new ball park John Henry Lloyd Stadium.

POP LLOYD

Henry "Hank" Aaron

BORN: FEBRUARY 5, 1934, MOBILE, ALABAMA
BATS: RIGHT / THROWS: RIGHT

Elected to the Baseball Hall of Fame in 1982

Before a spring training game in 1954, Ted Williams was having a conversation with a reporter over the monotonous cracks of batting practice behind them. Suddenly, a thunderclap jolted the legendary slugger and he spun around. "Who the hell hit that one?" he asked, his savvy ear still ringing. "That's that skinny kid the Braves just signed," the writer replied, "Aaron."

When he was thirteen, Hank's father took him to see Jackie Robinson, and the quiet youngster announced, "I'm gonna play ball with him." The Aarons couldn't afford equipment, so Hank used a mop handle to hit bottle caps pitched Frisbee-style by his brother. To top it off, because Hank had no coach, he held the stick cross-handed. This regimen must have been a recipe for the sharpest of batting eyes and the strongest of wrists, for it produced the greatest natural right-handed hitter in baseball history.

At sixteen Hank graduated to sandlot ball. Still hitting with his odd grip, but with a real bat and ball, he was a terror. A scout for the Memphis Black Bears saw Hank and offered him a fortune: ten bucks a game. He made the switch to semipro ball seamlessly. Then, on the last day of the 1951 season, the Indianapolis Clowns of the Negro American League came to town for an exhibition. They looked to breeze through the Bears, but the unassuming Aaron tore them up. One look was enough, and like Memphis had done to his sandlot team, the Clowns grabbed Hank from the Bears. But he was so shy and youthful that the rugged veterans elbowed him aside. He rode the bus and rode the pine. Finally, he got into a game up in Buffalo against the famous Kansas City Monarchs. The third professional pitch he saw he crushed onto a parkway behind left field, and "The Hammer" was born. Hank led the Negro American League in almost every category that year, and was seen by a scout for the Boston Braves.

As always, one look, or even one sound, was enough.

HENRY AARON

John Beckwith

BORN: JANUARY 7, 1900, LOUISVILLE, KENTUCKY
DIED: JANUARY 4, 1956
BATS: RIGHT / THROWS: RIGHT

Big John Beckwith bears remembering anytime the discussion turns to world-class power hitters. Born in 1900, he began playing professional ball in 1919 for the Chicago Giants. There he caught the eye of Rube Foster, who brought John over to his Chicago American Giants for the 1921 season. With Beckwith added to their already potent line-up—and playing several positions, including pitcher—Foster's Giants rolled to the Negro National League pennant, and then repeated as champs in 1922. Primarily known as a shortstop, Big John stayed with the Giants through 1924, the year in which he won the batting title with a .452 average and made the All-Star team as a catcher.

As player-manager for Harrisburg in 1927, Beckwith developed quite a rivalry with teammate Oscar Charleston. John edged Charleston's .335 average with his own .361, but lost out in homers 12-9 over sixty-nine games. The athletic 220-pound dead-pull hitter finished with a lifetime mark of .323 in the Negro Leagues and .337 against white Majors. He won back-to-back home run titles in 1930 and 1931. The great pitcher Willie Foster recalled, "If you made just one mistake to a man like Beckwith, just *one* wrong pitch—the ballgame was *over*."

Big John was an outspoken man with a hot temper, and differences of opinion kept him moving around the league from team to team. He played on ten ball clubs in all, including the Homestead Grays, Baltimore Black Sox, New York Black Yankees, Newark Dodgers, and the Brooklyn Royal Giants. Consequently, Beckwith probably holds the distinction of having hit more home runs for more teams than any other player in baseball history. Eventually his abrasive personality was exacerbated by an increasingly heavy drinking problem, until it outweighed his appeal as a player. By 1938, his welcome in the league was completely worn out.

JOHN BECKWITH

Martin Dihigo

BORN: MAY 25, 1905, MATANZAS, CUBA
DIED: MAY 20, 1971
BATS: RIGHT / THROWS: RIGHT

Elected to the Baseball Hall of Fame in 1977

In Cuba, he was known as "El Immortal." In Mexico, it was "El Maestro." And most of the players of the States who saw him in action agree with John McGraw that Martin Dihigo was "one of the greatest natural ballplayers *ever*."

Born in 1905 in Matanzas, fifty miles outside Havana, Dihigo was the first Cuban to reach Cooperstown. It has been said that in his country his name is the equivalent of Babe Ruth's or Joe DiMaggio's in America. The versatile 6'3", 220-pound phenom could have started at any position, with the possible exception of catcher, for any professional ball club throughout his remarkable 1923 to 1950 career. He is best remembered as an overpowering starting pitcher and a swift, graceful outfielder. On the hill, Martin posted a lifetime record of 256-136, relying on an exceptional fastball and a wicked breaking ball. In the outfield, he was a gifted gloveman known for his live, accurate arm and ability to throw out runners at home plate.

As a hitter, El Maestro batted over .400 on four occasions and finished with an average of .304. He was an excellent fastball hitter, and worked hard to overcome his early difficulty with the curve. He was capable of great power as well, once hitting a ball out of Greenlee Field in Pittsburgh onto a hospital roof 500 feet away. Dihigo had quite a year in 1942 as player-manager for Torreón in the Mexican League. He won twenty-two of the twenty-nine games he pitched, led in strikeouts and ERA, hit .319 and, with his club, won the pennant. Hall of Famer Buck Leonard, who played on some of the greatest teams in the Negro Leagues, said of Martin, "If he's not the greatest, I don't know who is."

MARTIN DIHIGO

Ernie Banks

BORN: JANUARY 31, 1931, DALLAS, TEXAS
BATS: RIGHT / THROWS: RIGHT

Elected to the Baseball Hall of Fame in 1977

When you catch the eye of none other than Cool Papa Bell, and he personally recommends you to Kansas City Monarchs manager Buck O'Neil, you know you're doing something special. When Buck, being the man that he was, realizes that you're too special to keep to himself in the dwindling Negro Leagues and personally recommends you to the Chicago Cubs, you know you have a shot at being a star. Ernie Banks was certainly a star.

Ernie was a well-rounded athlete in high school, playing football, basketball, and running track. He once ran the quarter mile in fifty-two seconds. Baseball was not yet on the youngster's mind, but his dad used to bribe him with a dime to have a catch, and oh, how that meager investment paid off. By the age of seventeen he was playing semipro ball around the Dallas area, earning fifteen dollars a game. To a black Texas teenager back in 1940s, it may have seemed like a fortune for doing something that he would have done all day for the love of it, but the sun was just peeking over the horizon on the fabulous career of this warmhearted *wunderkind*.

When Cool Papa saw Banks and brought him to the mighty Monarchs in 1950, they all got more than they had bargained for. The smiling shortstop was all that they had hoped for in the field, quickly becoming the best in the league, but the slim right-hander also turned out to be a bona fide world-class slugger. In 1953, with Ernie hitting for power and average, finishing at .347, and outshining all others at short, Buck O'Neil called the Cubs and told them that he had someone special.

Ernie Banks went on to have a storied career, winning back-to-back National League MVP awards in 1958 and 1959, playing in eleven All-Star Games, hitting 512 lifetime homers, and setting a new standard for shortstops. More important, "Mr. Cub" continues to get back the much-deserved love that he gives out to everyone he meets.

ERNIE BANKS

José Mendez

BORN: MARCH 19, 1887, CARDENAS, MATANZAS, CUBA
DIED: OCTOBER 31, 1928
BATS: RIGHT / THROWS: RIGHT

Elected to the Baseball Hall of Fame in 2006

José Mendez was known as "the black Christy Mathewson," but the astute John McGraw of the New York Giants once said, "He's more of a Walter Johnson and Grover Alexander rolled into one . . . and worth at least thirty-thousand dollars a year!" Born in Cuba in 1887, Mendez set pro ball on its ear in 1908 when, pitching for the Almendares Blues, he held the touring Cincinnati Reds scoreless for twenty-five innings over three games. The first game would have been a no-hitter, but Red second baseman Miller Huggins broke it up with a one-out single in the ninth inning.

The Cubans called José "El Diamante Negro" (The Black Diamond). He had a white-hot fastball and a hard-breaking curve, using his unusually long fingers to give the ball extra spin. In his first seven years, Mendez led the league in victories and shutouts five times. In 1909, José teamed with fellow Cuban League pitcher Eustaquiño Pedroso to whip the barnstorming Detroit Tigers, whose lineup included batting champ Ty Cobb and RBI king Sam Crawford; the Tigers staggered out of Cuba with a 4-8 record. That summer, José traveled to the States and compiled a record of 44-2. In 1910, he was 18-2. Mendez was still winning in 1914 when, without warning, his golden arm turned to lead. He dropped out of baseball for several years, but resurfaced in 1920 when the Negro National League was formed. As manager-shortstop on J. L. Wilkerson's new Kansas City Monarchs, José steered the team to three straight pennants from 1923 through 1925. In the 1924 World Series, he even gave himself the ball as starting pitcher in the deciding game, and at age thirty-six, like Lazarus reborn, pitched a shutout against the hard-hitting Hilldales. Tragically, five years later at the age of forty-one, José Mendez died of pneumonia.

JOSE MENDEZ

Max Manning

BORN: NOVEMBER 18, 1918, ROME, GEORGIA
DIED: JUNE 23, 2003
BATS: LEFT / THROWS: RIGHT

In 1937, the Detroit Tigers learned of a hot young pitching prospect in New Jersey. A rangy right-hander with a tricky sidearm delivery was mowin' 'em down for the semipro Camden Giants. But the scout returned home and no tryout was scheduled. The reason? Max Manning was black.

Max signed instead with the Newark Eagles in 1938. There, tagged "Dr. Cyclops" due to his heavy eyeglasses, he got a chance to play with such greats as Leon Day, Willie Wells, Monte Irvin, Ray Dandridge, and Mule Suttles. The youngster showed his stuff straight away when, in his first game, he struck out five Championship Homestead Grays, including Josh Gibson and Buck Leonard, to open the contest. Max settled nicely into the rotation for the next three years. He was a solid starter who rang up consecutive winning seasons before being drafted in 1942 and sent into the European theater, where he drove a gasoline truck that kept General Patton's Armored Third Army supplied through such meat grinders as the Battle of the Bulge and Bastogne.

Home in 1946, Max rejoined the Eagles and went 11-1, the one loss being his first game back. He finished second in the league in strikeouts only to teammate Leon Day, and the Eagles won the crown. That fall he played for Satchel Paige's All-Stars against Bob Feller's barnstorming club, striking out fourteen major leaguers in a 2-1 loss.

The New York Cubans signed Max in 1948, but in his first start he suffered a terrible shoulder tear. An operation proved little help, and despite posting a mark of 10-4 the next year, the pain was too much. Although many players were now entering the Majors, Max knew it was over.

After finishing his education at Glassboro State College, the bespectacled "Dr. Cyclops" finally looked the part of his profession. He spent the next twenty-eight years as a schoolteacher.

MAX MANNING

George "Mule" Suttles

BORN: MARCH 31, 1900, BLOCTON, ALABAMA
DIED: JULY 9, 1966
BATS: RIGHT / THROWS: RIGHT

Elected to the Baseball Hall of Fame in 2006

Buck Leonard, who hit behind Josh Gibson for a living, said "Mule Suttles was the hardest hitter I ever saw." Pitchers winced when Suttles strode to the plate with his fifty-ounce bat: chances were good the 6'6", 230-pound Louisiana-born first baseman would launch one of their offerings to five hundred feet dead center. Big George, who hit fastballs and curves alike, batted .320 in the Negro Leagues and .374 against white Major Leaguers. In 1926, he posted a league-leading average of .418 with an astounding slugging percentage of .830—and led in triples (nineteen) and homers (twenty-six). In his seventy-four at-bats against white Major League pitching, Suttles hit eleven home runs—an average of one every *seven* times up! Shortstop Willie Wells recalled a particularly prodigious Suttles blast in Cuba, at Havana's enormous Tropical Park. "I bet it was six hundred feet!" he exclaimed. "There was a wall five hundred feet away, and soldiers would patrol the top of it on horseback. Mule hit it *over* their heads."

Mule's greatest kick came in 1935. The All-Star Game was deadlocked 8-8 in the bottom of the eleventh. Hall of Famer Martin Dihigo was on the mound for the East. Cool Papa Bell led off for the West with a walk and was sacrificed to second. Josh Gibson was up, and Dihigo, seeing West hurler Willie Cornelius in the on-deck circle, intentionally walked the dangerous catcher. Suddenly Cornelius slipped back into the dugout, and out thundered the Mule. The only thing louder than Dihigo's heart pounding was the thousands of fans stomping their feet and screaming, "KICK, MULE, KICK!" With the count 1-1, Dihigo went to his fastball and Mule smashed a rocket deep into the centerfield bleachers. As he rounded third base, bedlam erupted—and the wildly cheering fans tore down the fences and poured onto the field.

MULE SUTTLES

Hilton Smith

BORN: FEBRUARY 27, 1907, GIDDINGS, TEXAS
DIED: NOVEMBER 18, 1983
BATS: RIGHT / THROWS: RIGHT

Elected to the Baseball Hall of Fame in 2001

Forever in Satchel Paige's colorful shadow, hurler Hilton Smith was the reserved yin to his more flamboyant teammate's yang. These equal forces working in concert propelled the Kansas City Monarchs to five pennants in the first six years of the Negro American Leagues' existence.

This temperate son of a schoolteacher was born in Giddings, Texas, in 1912. He pitched for Prairie View A&M College, then around the Negro Southern League for a few years. But it was in 1936 that the twenty-four-year-old right-hander joined the dynamic, barnstorming Kansas City Monarchs. It was to be his home for twelve successive, successful seasons.

Smith, who was regarded as having the sharpest curveball in the league, won over twenty games every year. But hitters couldn't look for that hook. He might throw an overhand fastball, a sinker, or even slip down sidearm and fire a slider anywhere in the count. Hilton hit his stride in 1937, tossing a no-hitter, and then rolled through the 1938 season without a single loss. Over a six-year stretch he racked up a 129-28 record and appeared in six All-Star Games. Smith held a 6-1 exhibition record over major leaguers. Playing winter ball in Venezuela, he faced the touring New York Yankees and one-hit them over five innings to get the 4-3 win.

There's no denying that Satchel Paige was the greatest draw in the Negro Leagues. To put fans in the seats, Satch would sometimes be slated to start every day. In order to keep from killing his golden arm, Paige often pitched an inning or three, and Hilton would often go the remainder in "relief." Incredibly, an off day might be spent playing first base, the outfield, or because he was adept with the bat, pinch-hitting. By the time Smith was thirty-five, he felt the toll. When Jackie Robinson broke the color line, the Brooklyn Dodgers offered Hilton a deal, but the proud hurler did not want to be finally introduced to millions of fans at a time when he knew that his greatest playing days were behind him. He declined, and like his father, became a teacher.

HILTON SMITH

Ben Taylor

BORN: JULY 1, 1888, ANDERSON, SOUTH CAROLINA
DIED: JANUARY 24, 1953
BATS: LEFT / THROWS: LEFT

Elected to the Baseball Hall of Fame in 2006

Ben Taylor came from an illustrious baseball family. His brother, Charles "C. I." Taylor, was the manager of the strong Indianapolis ABCs. Another brother, "Candy Jim" Taylor, was a well-respected third baseman who went on to become vice-chairman of the Negro National League. Still *another* brother, "Steel Arm" Johnny Taylor, was a star pitcher on five different teams. But as a player, Ben was by far the family's best. He was one of the top first basemen ever to come out of black ball.

Ben began his career in 1914 with the Chicago American Giants, but in 1915 moved over to his brother C. I.'s Indianapolis ABCs, where he remained for the next seven years. He built a reputation as a "heads-up" fielder, with a fine glove and excellent throwing arm. The South Carolina-born lefty was a standout hitter who, while not noted for his power, could drive the ball to all fields and occasionally stretch a single into extra bases. He finished his Negro Leagues playing career with a very respectable .333 lifetime average. In the 1952 *Pittsburgh Courier* All-Star poll, Ben was named, along with Buck Leonard and Jud Wilson, as one of the three best black first basemen of all time.

While mastering the physical aspects of baseball, Ben also paid careful attention to the subtleties of the game, and he later employed this knowledge as a top-notch manager. In fact, as owner-manager of the Baltimore Stars, Ben Taylor is credited with helping mold the career of Hall of Fame first baseman Buck Leonard. Buck was quick to pay homage to Ben, calling him "one of the greatest first basemen in colored history." Some of the teams Taylor graced include the Bacharach Giants, the Baltimore Black Sox, and the Brooklyn Eagles.

BEN TAYLOR

Willard Brown

BORN: JUNE 26, 1915, SHREVEPORT, LOUISIANA
DIED: AUGUST 4, 1996
BATS: RIGHT / THROWS: RIGHT

Elected to the Baseball Hall of Fame in 2006

"Home Run" Brown could have been a baseball hero. He could run like a leopard, make catches in center field that stunned opponents, and his power at the plate was on a par with Gibson's, Suttles's, and Stearnes's. Willard didn't just hit balls out of parks, he hit them over the buildings *behind* the parks. The Shreveport-born 6', 200-pound right-hander claimed ten home run titles and four batting crowns in a twenty-two-year career covering 1935 to 1956. His lifetime average was .342 in black ball and .364 against white big leaguers. He set a record in Puerto Rico with twenty-seven home runs in sixty games. An impatient free-swinger who never waited for strikes, Brown often hit balls over his head for homers—and once, in Birmingham, he hit a pitch that bounced in the dirt in front of the plate up and over the left field fence.

To Willard, hitting home runs was like shooting ducks in a barrel, but with his strange behavior, he shot *himself* in the foot. He got a reputation with the Kansas City Monarchs as a "lackadaisical" player with a "bad attitude" by occasionally allowing long fly balls to land at the wall without chasing them, letting the hitter score—and then denying responsibility for what he called a "pitcher's mistake." Some days he displayed world-class speed, but other times he'd just "trot" or "loaf" in the outfield and on the bases.

After Jackie Robinson broke the color line, Willard—then thirty-five years old but hitting .425—was signed by the St. Louis Browns. He promptly smashed the first homer a black man ever hit in the American League, but then seemed to "stop caring," and his average fell to .179. Cut from St. Louis, Willard Brown finished out his career in the Texas League, never tasting the full fame and recognition he might have had.

WILLARD BROWN

Andrew "Rube" Foster

BORN: SEPTEMBER 17, 1879, CALVERT, TEXAS
DIED: DECEMBER 9, 1930
BATS: RIGHT / THROWS: RIGHT

Elected to the Baseball Hall of Fame in 1981

As the Cuban X-Giants' star pitcher in 1902, Rube Foster won fifty-one games and took four out of five from the Philadelphia Giants to capture the "Colored World Championship." He then switched to those same Philadelphia Giants in 1903, and pitched *them* to the championship. Honus Wagner called Foster "the smoothest pitcher I've ever seen," and he is credited with teaching Christy Mathewson the screwball. But it is not for his pitching that Rube Foster is best remembered. It is for his great vision.

In 1910, the Texas-born Foster formed his own club, the Chicago American Giants. He built powerful teams based on speed and pitching, teams that would dominate the next decade. A master strategist, he invented plays the white Major Leaguers had never seen before, such as the hit-and-run bunt.

Then, seeing the effects poor conditions and poorer pay had on other black clubs, Foster created the Negro National League in 1920 and, as president, he ran it like the Majors. He increased interest and attendance by holding organized pennant races and introducing All-Star Games, raised equipment standards, and assured players regular paychecks for set amounts—while drawing no salary himself. Foreseeing the eventual end to racial segregation, Foster counseled his athletes to maintain a high level of play. "When the doors are opened, you must be ready to walk through," was his advice. But holding the National Negro League's eight teams together single-handedly while continuing to manage his own American Giants proved too much for Rube. He suffered a nervous breakdown in 1926 and, within a few short years, was gone.

The visionary Andrew "Rube" Foster, "Father of Black Baseball," was elected to the Baseball Hall of Fame in 1981.

RUBE FOSTER

Leroy "Satchel" Paige

BORN: JULY 7, 1906, MOBILE, ALABAMA
DIED: JUNE 8, 1982
BATS: RIGHT / THROWS: RIGHT

Elected to the Baseball Hall of Fame in 1971

Every once in a great while an athlete comes along with that rare blend of awesome talent and charismatic appeal that swells ballparks with thousands of fans—fans not there to see a game, but to witness an individual live up to his legend *again*. Satchel Paige was just such a magical man.

In 1926, hapless hitters began fanning on Satchel's blazing fastball, and forty years later, their luck hadn't changed. For twenty-nine of those years, 1929–58, he played both summer *and* winter ball. In one year alone, he pitched in 153 games, pitching every day for a week or even a month as a matter of course. The long, lean, rubber-armed right-hander was the winningest hurler in the history of the Negro Leagues, and probably in baseball anywhere.

Satchel estimated that by 1961 he had taken the mound 2,500 times, won 2,000 games, and thrown 100 no-hitters. He achieved a career-high twenty-two strikeouts in a single game on several occasions, including once in 1930 against a team of white Major Leaguers. Relying mainly on a phenomenally accurate fastball (called his "Bee-Ball," because it buzzed), Paige confused hitters by mixing up his delivery, becoming known as the "Man of a Thousand Wind-ups." His famous "Hesitation Pitch" was so destructive to batters' timing that it was ruled illegal by the American League.

In 1948, Satchel became the first black man to pitch in the American League, as well as the oldest rookie at forty-two, and his appearances set attendance records for the Cleveland Indians. He was 6-1 that year, and the Indians won the World Series. In 1965, at the age of fifty-nine, the grand old fireballer pitched his last three innings in the big leagues for the Kansas City Athletics, allowing just one hit.

SATCHEL PAIGE

Spottswood "Spot" Poles

BORN: DECEMBER 9, 1887, WINCHESTER, VIRGINIA
DIED: SEPTEMBER 12, 1962
BATS: BOTH / THROWS: RIGHT

The legendary performer and social activist Paul Robeson once said that the four greatest black athletes he had ever seen were, "Jack Johnson, Joe Louis, Jesse Owens . . . and Spot Poles." The first three are world famous, because boxing and the Olympics were not segregated. But, unfortunately for Spot . . .

Standing 5'7" and weighing 165 pounds, this heavily muscled Virginian was a deadball dynamo. He had slashing speed, and ran the 100-yard dash in under ten seconds. Spot covered vast stretches of center field like a shot, and was a terror on the bases. In 1911, this switch-hitting lead-off man stole forty-one sacks in the first sixty games he played for the New York Lincoln Giants. In his first four seasons he ripped for averages of .440, .398, .414, and .487! Poles especially tore up Major League pitching in exhibitions, hitting an obscene .594, including three straight hits off of the great Grover Cleveland Alexander. New York Giants manager John McGraw swore that if there were no color line, Spot Poles would be in the top four to sign a contract in the Majors.

Spot had the heart of a lion. Mid-career he joined the army and served in WWI as a sergeant in the 369th Infantry. He saw heavy fighting and won five battle stars and a purple heart. But while he may have been A1 wearing the uniform of his country on a battlefield, back home his skin color still made him "unfit" to wear a Major League uniform on a ball field. He then toured with a team of black servicemen called the Hellfighters, as their player/manager, before returning to the Lincoln Giants.

Spot retired in 1923. Having been smart about money, he purchased a small fleet of taxis with his savings, and lived quite comfortably. He indulged a lifelong love of horse racing, and was a perennial fixture at the Kentucky Derby. He even coached a semipro ball club, and at the age of sixty penciled himself in for old time's sake and got a pinch-hit single.

Spot Poles is buried at Arlington National Cemetery.

SPOT POLES

Cristobal Torriente

BORN: NOVEMBER 16, 1893, CIENFUEGOS, CUBA
DIED: APRIL 11, 1938
BATS: LEFT / THROWS: LEFT

Elected to the Baseball Hall of Fame in 2006

A big, good-natured lefty known as the "Cuban Strongman," Cristobal Torriente was a walking ball club. Widely believed to have been the best right fielder in the Negro Leagues, he was blessed with sure hands, the speed to get under any drive, and a riflelike arm. He was also an excellent second baseman, amazingly good at third for a southpaw, and a winning pitcher with a record of 15-5. To top it off, Torri was one of the finest hitters in any league.

Cristobal, a notorious "bad ball" hitter, had the control to spray the ball to all fields, but is best remembered for his power swing. Playing for the Chicago American Giants, he regularly hit line drives over the 400-foot mark on the center field wall. Shortstop Bob Williams recalled that when the Giants visited Kansas City, Torri hit a line drive that cracked a clock seventeen feet over the center field fence, and "the hands just started goin' 'round and 'round!" In 1920, while Cristobal was in Cuba with the Havana Reds, the New York Giants came to town, bringing with them none other than Babe Ruth. In one game, Torriente homered in his first two at-bats, and came up for the third time with two men on base. Ruth, who'd been a top-notch starting pitcher in Boston, trotted in from right field and demanded to pitch to him. Torri promptly stroked a two-run double, and although Ruth then struck out three in a row, the Babe was back in the outfield next inning. Later, Torri amazingly slugged his *third* homer of the game. Back in the U.S., his clutch home run won the deciding game of the 1921 Negro Leagues World Series for the Chicago American Giants.

In a career that spanned 1913 to 1934, Torriente earned a .339 average against black pitching, .311 against white Major Leaguers, and the respect of everyone who watched him play.

CRISTOBAL TORRIENTE

James Raleigh "Biz" Mackey

BORN: JULY 27, 1897, EAGLE PASS, TEXAS
DIED: SEPTEMBER 22, 1965
BATS: BOTH / THROWS: RIGHT

Elected to the Baseball Hall of Fame in 2006

The most famous catcher in the Negro Leagues was Josh Gibson, but who was the best? Experts agree that while Josh was a fine catcher, and certainly the greatest slugger, no one, but *no* one, was the artist and master behind the plate that Biz Mackey was. Hall of Famer Roy Campanella credited Mackey for having "taught me everything I know," and stated flatly, "Biz was the defensive master of *all* catchers."

The happy-go-lucky Texan began his pro career in 1918 with the San Antonio Black Aces, but spent the bulk of his twenty years in baseball with the Philadelphia Stars. In 1927, he played several exhibition games in Japan, where his good nature and hard work ethic won the hearts of the foreign fans. Yet as great as he was behind the dish, Biz was a fine, consistent performer alongside it as well. He posted a lifetime average of .319, and hit .326 against white Major Leaguers. Finishing out his career in 1945 with the Newark Eagles, Biz could still deliver. Club owner Effa Manley remembered, "If it was late in the game and we needed just one hit, he was over fifty, but it was Mackey who got it."

Monte Irvin called Biz "the dean of all teachers" for the way he handled young pitchers. "He made good pitchers great." Judy Johnson raved about the way he threw out base runners: "You wouldn't have to move that glove six inches; he put the ball down there on a dime. He threw fast but *light*; you could have caught it bare-handed!" Don Newcombe said, "Biz was one of the most knowledgeable baseball men ever." And at the Los Angeles Coliseum tribute to Roy Campanella in 1959, Campy insisted Biz stand beside him and accept the applause of 90,000 adoring fans.

Dobie Moore

BORN: JANUARY 9, 1895, ATLANTA, GEORGIA
DIED: DECEMBER 1, 1977
BATS: RIGHT / THROWS: RIGHT

At a solid 230 pounds, with long muscular arms and lightning reflexes, this big cat was a born athlete. Dobie Moore may have been built to play linebacker in George Halas's fledgling NFL, but instead he prowled the infield as the star shortstop for the Kansas City Monarchs in the early 1920s.

A rifle-armed righty with astounding range, Moore got his start in baseball on the 25th Infantry team, and then was brought to the attention of the Monarchs by Casey Stengel. Dobie signed with them in 1920 and began establishing himself as a top player in the newly formed Negro National League. By 1923 Moore was firing on all cylinders, making incredible defensive plays in the field and batting cleanup in the order. He then powered the Monarchs to three straight pennants by hitting .365, .453, and .325 over that stretch. He batted .300 in the 1924 World Series win over Hilldale, and the next year hit .364 and led in hits, RBI, and slugging percentage. The young star jumped out to another searing start in 1926, but a dark day lay ahead for Dobie in Detroit.

One evening early that season, Moore arranged to meet three of his teammates at a nightclub, but the shortstop never arrived. En route, Dobie decided to stop and see a woman he knew in town, Elise Brown. The motive for what transpired next is lost to the fog of time, but whether she mistook Moore for a burglar, or there was a quarrel of some kind, Ms. Brown drew a pistol and pulled the trigger. Dobie was struck in the leg, and as Elise leveled her revolver again, he leapt from the balcony to avoid the shot. But with the burning lead wedged deep in his leg bone, when Moore hit the alley floor his limb shattered irreparably, and with it, the promising career of this natural-born ballplayer.

DOBIE MOORE

Bruce Petway

BORN: 1883, NASHVILLE, TENNESSEE
DIED: JULY 4, 1941
BATS: BOTH / THROWS: RIGHT

Little Bruce Petway, affectionately known as "Buddy," set the defensive standard that all Negro League catchers would strive for. Starting his professional career in 1906, he provided influence and inspiration for the highly acclaimed Biz Mackey, who in turn molded the careers of a host of exceptional black backstops including Roy Campanella. Buddy and Biz were undoubtedly the greatest defensive catchers never to play in the Majors.

Petway fell in love with baseball while attending Meharry Medical College in Nashville, Tennessee, around the turn of the century. He started out with the Leland Giants, but moved to Sol White's Philadelphia club in 1907, where he helped them defeat Rube Foster's Lelands in four straight games. So impressed was Foster that he bought Petway from the Phillies and retained him for over ten years. Bruce is best remembered as the rock-solid anchor behind home on Foster's Chicago American Giants, where he stayed from 1911 until his retirement in 1919.

Buddy had a terrific throwing arm and possessed pinpoint accuracy. Playing winter ball for the Havana Reds in 1910, he faced Major League base-stealing champ Ty Cobb of the Detroit Tigers in five games. Petway worked out a plan with shortstop Pop Lloyd, calling for Buddy to throw the ball three feet to the first base side of second and two feet behind the bag. Cobb went 0-3 trying to steal: Bruce put the ball out there on a dime and Lloyd tagged the immortal "Georgia Peach" as he sped past, thus avoiding Cobb's legendary spikes. In his final attempt, Cobb saw the throw had him beat and just walked off the field. Petway also outhit Cobb (the American League batting champ that year) .390 to .371 over the series.

Bruce later managed the Detroit Stars from 1919 to 1925.

BRUCE PETWAY

Monte Irvin

BORN: FEBRUARY 25, 1919, COLUMBIA, ALABAMA
BATS: RIGHT / THROWS: RIGHT

Elected to the Baseball Hall of Fame in 1973

Monte Irvin is a name known and respected by baseball fans everywhere. The strong right-hander had a marvelous eight-year career with the New York Giants of the National League, starting in 1948. In 1951, Monte hit .312 with twenty-four home runs to lead the Giants to the World Series. In 1954, he hit .329 with twenty-one homers to take them back again. He finished with a lifetime Major League average of .293 and ninety-nine home runs. But what many fans don't realize is that before coming to the Majors, Monte spent eleven years, his *prime* years, with the Newark Eagles of the Negro Leagues.

Monte, a 6'1", 195-pound left fielder, began his pro career with the Eagles in 1938. He had great speed and a powerful throwing arm, could charge or go back on line drives with the best, and always got a good jump on the ball. An all-around player with sharp defensive skills, he also logged time at shortstop and third base. But it was his offense, his swing, that opponents feared most of all. Monte hit .395 in 1941 to take the Negro League batting title, but then missed the next four years to serve in WWII. He came back in 1946 to hit .394, again take the crown, and put the Eagles in the Black World Series. Over the seven hotly contested games, Irvin hit .462 with three home runs to lift Newark over the Kansas City Monarchs, 4-3. Monte's .373 Negro Leagues lifetime average is among the highest ever recorded.

Monte Irvin was and is a tremendously well-liked individual. Many people at the time felt he would have been a better choice than Jackie Robinson as the first black man in the Majors. In 1968, Irvin accepted a request from the Commissioner's Office to work in public relations, and is truly one of baseball's "ambassadors of good will."

MONTE IRVIN

Oscar Charleston

BORN: OCTOBER 14, 1896, INDIANAPOLIS, INDIANA
DIED: OCTOBER 5, 1954
BATS: LEFT / THROWS: LEFT

Elected to the Baseball Hall of Fame in 1976

When the baseball gods create the perfect player, they pour in ample portions of raw power and stunning speed. Add to that talent, style, dedication, concentration, and a mighty measure of lifelong fiery enthusiasm, and the results are truly awesome. Old-timers and experts often argue who was the best pitcher, catcher, infielder, or outfielder, and who hit the farthest or ran the fastest. But ask who was the greatest all-around player in the Negro Leagues, and the chant goes up for Charleston.

The rugged southpaw center fielder with the intense gray eyes could do it all. The 1921 season alone saw this one-man wrecking crew win the batting crown with a .434 average, and also lead the league in doubles, triples, homers, and stolen bases. Charleston's lifetime average is .357, and he tagged top white pitching for .326.

Oscar, who started his career with his hometown Indianapolis ABCs in 1915, was known as "The Black Ty Cobb." (It's a comparison thought by many as generous to "The Georgia Peach.") While the men boasted similar plate performances, Charleston sported superior leather in the field. Playing remarkably shallow to steal singles, on well-hit balls he would spin at the crack of the bat and race deep to make eye-popping circus catches. Dave Malarcher claimed that the right and left fielders "just played the lines and caught foul balls. Oscar handled the rest." On high fly balls he couldn't resist a little showmanship, waiting until the last second to whip out his glove for the "snap-catch," or hauling it in behind his back.

Later in his twenty-seven year career, the charismatic Charleston moved to first base and became player-manager of the Pittsburgh Crawfords during their powerhouse years of 1932–38. Oscar still hit over .300 each year, and was elected to the All-Star Game three times at his new position. He then managed the Philadelphia Stars for nearly ten more years, and advised Brooklyn Dodger owner Branch Rickey about which black players should be given consideration for the Major Leagues.

OSCAR CHARLESTON

Leon Day

BORN: OCTOBER 30, 1916, ALEXANDRIA, VIRGINIA
DIED: MARCH 13, 1995
BATS: RIGHT / THROWS: RIGHT

Elected to the Baseball Hall of Fame in 1995

Leon Day was known for being extremely humble and soft-spoken. His fastball, however, wasn't. It would split your mitt.

Day, a 5'7", 140-pound right-hander, began pitching in 1934 for the Bacharach Giants, but came into fame as a power pitcher for the Newark Eagles in the 1940s. In 1942, Leon captured the official Negro Leagues' single-game strikeout record by fanning eighteen with his heater and curve. The only hit that afternoon was a leadoff bloop single to left; among Day's victims was Roy Campanella, who was rung up three times. Shortly thereafter, Leon entered military service and lost the next few years to WWII. When he returned to baseball in 1946, he announced his arrival by throwing a no-hitter in his first outing. That year, despite nursing a sore arm for most of the second half of the season, Day pitched the Eagles to a World Series victory over the Kansas City Monarchs, whose starting pitcher was Satchel Paige.

Leon was a versatile performer who also played second base and the outfield in his twenty-two-year career. He was a switch-hitter who was consistently around the .300 mark. One time, Day was locked in a 0-0 pitching battle with his old rival, Satchel Paige. Leon settled matters by homering off Satch in the ninth inning to score the game's only run and pocket the victory. Day won three out of four starts against Paige, and his seven East-West All-Star Game appearances stand as a record for the Negro Leagues.

On March 7, 1995, Leon Day received the call that ballplayers dream of from boyhood: he had been elected to the hallowed halls of Cooperstown. "I never thought it would come," said the tearful, seventy-eight-year-old Day. Leon passed away six days later, at peace, knowing that he was one of the greatest . . . and that now the world knew too.

LEON DAY

John Donaldson

BORN: FEBRUARY 20, 1892, GLASGOW, MISSOURI
DIED: APRIL 14, 1970
BATS: LEFT / THROWS: LEFT

John Donaldson began pitching professionally in 1912 for a barnstorming midwestern team known as the Tennessee Rats. The Rats may not have been a serious club, but Donaldson was a *serious* left-hander. His ability was recognized by club owner J. L. Wilkinson, who brought John to his solid All-Nations club in 1916, and made him the team's star starter for the next four years. In 1920, Rube Foster asked Wilkinson to form a Kansas City team for the new Negro National League, and it was Donaldson who suggested the name "Monarchs."

The tall, lank, Missouri-born Donaldson is best remembered for his "outpitch," a sharp-breaking curveball he could throw for a strike anywhere in the count, with the velocity of most pitchers' fastballs. John rang up twenty strikeouts in a single game many times, and once threw three consecutive no-hitters. Major League manager John McGraw said that if he could have signed a black man, he would have signed Donaldson for $50,000.

When John began to age as a pitcher, he spent many years in the latter part of his career playing for the Monarchs in the outfield and, seeing action on a daily basis, established himself as a reliable hitter. But Donaldson longed to return to his first love, the hill. When he eventually left Kansas City, he moved to Minnesota, where he pitched for Little Falls, a semipro team in the Northwestern League. There, the aging Donaldson went up against many young arms bound for fame in the Negro Leagues, and remained a winning pitcher.

When experts were assembled in 1952 to choose the *Pittsburgh Courier* All-Star team, they picked Donaldson as one of the best black left-handers of all time.

JOHN DONALDSON

Dave Brown

BORN: 1896, SAN MARCOS, TEXAS
DIED: UNKNOWN
BATS: LEFT / THROWS: LEFT

The story of Dave Brown is one of the most mysterious in all of sports. Dave was perhaps the most talented left-handed pitcher of his day, and many agree with expert third baseman and manager David Malarcher, who claimed, "Brown could have been the best black pitcher ever." But something was tragically wrong with Dave Brown. He just couldn't straighten himself out.

Brown started pitching professionally for Rube Foster's Chicago American Giants in 1918, but only after Rube posted a twenty-thousand-dollar bond to get Dave out of prison. Brown repaid Foster by pitching the American Giants to three World Championships in 1920, 1921, and 1922. One of the championship games in 1921 was an extraordinary pitchers' duel between Brown and "Cannonball" Dick Redding of the Bacharachs. Redding threw a no-hitter through six innings, as Brown held the powerful Bacharachs to a single run. Redding ran out of gas, but Dave hung tough and eventually got the 3-1 complete game victory.

In 1923, the Eastern Colored League was formed, and the "player wars" broke out, with the new East stealing talent from the established West. Dave Brown abandoned Rube Foster and signed with the Lincoln Giants. Foster sorely missed Brown in his starting rotation, and the American Giants managed no better than third place that year. But Brown's year with the Lincolns was to be his last in baseball. In 1924, sought by police in connection with a homicide over a cocaine deal in New York, he just seemed to vanish into thin air. Some old-timers say he was found dead in California with his throat slashed, others claim to have seen him alive and well in the Midwest. The only thing we know for sure concerning Dave Brown is that his was a wasted talent.

DAVE BROWN

Dick Lundy

BORN: JULY 10, 1898, JACKSONVILLE, FLORIDA
DIED: JANUARY 5, 1965
BATS: BOTH / THROWS: RIGHT

When an aging Pop Lloyd finally abdicated the throne of "King of Black Shortstops," his crown was assumed by a young switch-hitting sensation out of Florida named Dick Lundy.

This right-hander was a graceful man with large muscular hands. His throws to first base were like most pitchers' fastballs. Lundy had terrific speed and range, and made breathtaking plays deep in the hole. He had a reputation as a man who "could throw you out at first from left field." King Richard was a fierce competitor. If a friend or teammate moved to a rival club, he could be expected to be tagged out hard to the face or, if Lundy was running, even spiked. It was not out of mean-spiritedness, but because the game was the game, and he was respected for it.

Dick Lundy had a long association with the Bacharach Giants starting in 1916. He had tremendous years, playing a flawless short, hitting in the .300s, and was later in his tenure their player/manager. But in 1929, he moved over to perform those duties for the Baltimore Black Sox. There he rounded out the "Million Dollar Infield" with Oliver Marcelle, Frank Warfield, and Jud Wilson. It was the finest ever assembled, and they cruised to the championship. Lundy wound up his career with a lifetime .330 average, clubbed Major Leaguers for .344, and hit .341 in the Cuban winter leagues.

The famous manager of the New York Giants, John McGraw, kept a close eye on the Negro Leagues and desperately wanted to someday be able to sign players from there. In his opinion King Richard was, "with the exception of Honus Wagner, the greatest shortstop who ever lived."

DICK LUNDY

Grant "Home Run" Johnson

BORN: SEPTEMBER 21, 1874, FINDLAY, OHIO
DIED: SEPTEMBER 4, 1964
BATS: RIGHT / THROWS: RIGHT

One of the biggest sensations of the black deadball era was the power-swinging, baritone-singing shortstop known as "Home Run" Johnson.

In the year 1894, this raw-boned, right-handed rookie ripped an incredible sixty home runs for the semipro Findlay Sluggers. At the tender age of twenty, Grant had earned himself a nickname that he would carry throughout his career. Johnson was a clean-living physical fitness enthusiast. He was religious about his regimen long before it was fashionable, and his deadball homers were of the screaming line drive, run all day variety. He was patient at the plate, slick in the field, and performed like a seasoned pro right from the start. The very next year he formed the Page Fence Giants, and as their shortstop and captain hit .471 over a 154-game season in which the Giants went 118-34.

By the turn of the century, the Page Fence Giants were no more, but Home Run was going strong. After a stint with the Cuban X-Giants, where he won a championship in 1903, Johnson swung over to the Philadelphia Giants and collected two more crowns in 1905 and 1906. Johnson then joined the Brooklyn Royal Giants, was again elected team captain, and by 1909 had secured a title for them. Everywhere he went he was a leader and a winner. That winter he captained the Havana Reds in the Cuban League, and caused a ruckus when he outhit both Ty Cobb and "Wahoo" Sam Crawford of the Detroit Tigers.

Later in his career, Home Run played and managed mostly in upstate New York. His patience at the plate was matched by his manner with young players, who affectionately changed his nickname to "Dad." He was an excellent instructor who was always quick with a humorous saying or a stirring song with his rich, strong voice.

HOME RUN JOHNSON

Oliver "Ghost" Marcelle

BORN: JUNE 21,1895, THIBODAUX, LOUISIANA
DIED: JUNE 12, 1949
BATS: RIGHT / THROWS: RIGHT

One of the all-time best third basemen in black ball was the fiercely competitive Oliver Marcelle. He was willing to lose only one thing—his temper. In his twelve-year career spanning 1919 to 1930, the highly flammable Creole took on all comers, including the "Leagues' Toughest Man," Oscar Charleston. In an onfield brawl, Marcelle once cracked a bat over Oscar's head.

Though many described his play as "marvelous" and "graceful," other adjectives such as "violent," "wild," or "nasty" haunted the Ghost throughout his career.

The handsome right-hander from Thibodaux, Louisiana, with a love for winning, really was a marvelous performer. The famous 1952 *Pittsburgh Courier* poll named him the best black third baseman ever. Hall of Famer Judy Johnson, thought by many to be the best at third himself, said, "Marcelle was just wonderful. He made all the tough plays look easy." Marcelle had nerves of steel, would play in at almost bunt-depth on even the hardest hitters, and excelled at spearing line drives. This hotheaded hot cornerman hit to all fields, was at his best in clutch situations, and finished with a .310 lifetime average.

In 1929, the Baltimore Black Sox boasted hard-slugging Jud Wilson at first base, player-manager Frank Warfield at second, the sensational Dick Lundy at short, and with Marcelle at third, they sailed to the American League pennant. But this was to be the Ghost's last glory. That winter, a dice game turned ugly when Marcelle's infamous anger exploded and he attacked teammate Frank Warfield. In the vicious brawl that ensued, Warfield bit off Marcelle's nose. The swaggering Marcelle, a dapper ladies' man, was psychologically destroyed. The following year the Ghost appeared in only four games, and then faded from the Negro Leagues forever.

OLIVER MARCELLE

CF

Willie Mays

BORN: MAY 6, 1931, WESTFIELD, ALABAMA
BATS: RIGHT / THROWS: RIGHT

Elected to the Baseball Hall of Fame in 1979

In the most famous footage in World Series history, Willie Mays made what has ever since been known as "The Catch." It was an over-the-shoulder grab on the dead run of Cleveland slugger Vic Wertz's smash, some 415 feet from home plate. Willie then whirled and fired a rocket back to the infield and held the runners! But it is not inconceivable to think that Wertz might never have been robbed that day. It could quite possibly, instead, have been all of us.

"The Catch" occurred in 1954, the same year this nation's highest court was arguing *Brown v. Board of Education.* It wasn't until ten years later that the Civil Rights Act passed, declaring Jim Crow laws unconstitutional. If Jackie Robinson and Branch Rickey had not personally confronted baseball's segregation when they did, but rather waited for the Supreme Court to do so, we may well have never known, or believed, the unquestionable splendor of Willie Mays.

Willie started out as a sandlot shortstop for the Fairfield Stars, then went semipro for the Chattanooga Choo-Choos. In 1948, a year after Robinson broke into the Majors, Mays joined the Birmingham Black Barons of the Negro Leagues, and followed in his father, "Cat" Mays's, footsteps by switching to center field. Two years later he leaped into the Majors with the New York Giants and began a career so diversely incredible that it forever changed what it was thought possible to expect from any one player.

If, judging by much of the rest of the country, things had broken in baseball later than they did, Willie would have joined the Negro leaguers in forced obscurity. He might now be dismissed as a myth, rather than recognized as a legend. Instead, he stands as Exhibit A against any who would compound the crime by discounting the deeds of the many other diamond immortals depicted in these pages simply because they toiled at a time when most of their fellow countrymen callously chose to look away. For eternity, fans can only imagine the highlight reels of the incredible lives of these players and grieve, knowing that because of race, the cameras never rolled.

WILLIE MAYS

Smokey Joe Williams

BORN: APRIL 6, 1886, SEGUIN, TEXAS
DIED: FEBRUARY 25, 1951
BATS: RIGHT / THROWS: RIGHT

Elected to the Baseball Hall of Fame in 1999

"Someone gave me a baseball at an early age and it was my companion for a long time. I carried it in my pocket, and I slept with it under my pillow. I *always* wanted to pitch," said "Smokey" Joe Williams. And pitch he did. Williams was one of the greatest in baseball history.

Smokey Joe, a.k.a. "Cyclone Joe" or "Yank," began his career around the turn of the century, so many of his numbers are lost to antiquity. Though the fireballer's record is incomplete, some of the individual years available indicate his ability. He was 28-4 in 1905; 20-2 in 1908, and 32-8 in 1909. His best year was 1914, when he went 41-3 for the Chicago American Giants. He was 20-7 in the games he pitched against major leaguers. In 1917, Joe no-hit the pennant-winning New York Giants, fanning twenty, but lost on a tenth-inning error. That same year, he outdueled the great Walter Johnson 1-0. As late as 1930, a forty-five-year-old Smokey smoked twenty-five Kansas City Monarchs in a twelve-inning tilt against the doctored ball dandy Chet Brewer.

Those who saw the 6'5", 205-pound right-hander readily attest to his greatness. Williams was in his forties by the time Satchel Paige swore, "That Joe throws harder than anyone!" Dizzy Dean called old Yank's fastball "Lively an' agitatin'." The half Native American from Texas with the intimidating overhand delivery made his heater look downright laser-like by employing an excellent curve and changeup. Ty Cobb, not a man known to heap praise, flatly stated, "He'd be a sure thirty-game winner in the Majors."

Smokey Joe defeated seven Hall of Fame pitchers in his twenty-seven-year career, and in 1952 was voted "Best Black Pitcher of All Time," edging out Satchel Paige by one vote.

SMOKEY JOE WILLIAMS

Walter "Buck" Leonard

BORN: SEPTEMBER 8, 1907, ROCKY MOUNT, NORTH CAROLINA
DIED: NOVEMBER 27, 1997
BATS: LEFT / THROWS: LEFT

Elected to the Baseball Hall of Fame in 1972

Josh Gibson, known as "The Black Babe Ruth," was the Negro Leagues' most prolific home run slugger. Pitchers didn't want to challenge him, but they couldn't risk walking him either. He had what every great hitter needs: great protection in the lineup. He had Buck Leonard.

Buck Leonard was himself known as "The Black Lou Gehrig," and the similarities between the two hard-hitting lefties are many. While other men bounced around the league playing for many different teams, Leonard was the Homestead Grays' starting first baseman for a solid seventeen years, the same amount of time the "Iron Horse" logged at that position with the Yankees. Like Gehrig, who hit behind Ruth, it was the left-handed Leonard's responsibility to bat cleanup behind the most fabled long-ball threat to his league. Both men were among the classiest, well-liked, and respected players ever to grace the diamond.

Leonard, born in Rocky Mount, North Carolina, started playing organized ball in 1935 for sixty cents a day, but slugged his way up to become the third-highest-paid black player behind Satchel Paige and Josh Gibson. By 1948, Leonard was earning ten thousand dollars annually, including his winter ball pay from Durango in the Mexican League. The 5'11", 185-pound dead-pull fastball hitter had a high homer mark of forty-two in 1942, and averaged thirty-four each year. His personal best batting average, an incredible .492, came in 1939. He hit over .400 many times, and finished with a career .355. Buck was selected to twelve All-Star teams and, with Gibson, led the Grays to nine straight Negro National League pennants. Leonard retired at the age of forty-eight in 1950.

BUCK LEONARD

Jackie Roosevelt Robinson

BORN: JANUARY 31, 1919, CAIRO, GEORGIA
DIED: OCTOBER 24, 1972
BATS: RIGHT / THROWS: RIGHT

Elected to the Baseball Hall of Fame in 1962

Although his time in the Negro leagues was brief, Jackie Robinson was the slugging, sliding, shot heard 'round the world. He was Dr. King in cleats, who not so much lifted black players up, as exposed the insanity of their exclusion.

Jackie was born in 1919 in Georgia, but grew up in Pasadena, California. In 1939 he attended UCLA, where he was an excellent student, an All-American in football, and lettered in track and baseball. After college, Robinson joined the army. A lieutenant, he counted on fighting overseas, but found himself battling racism at home. After refusing to sit in the rear of a bus, he was court-martialed, later acquitted, and honorably discharged.

In 1945, Jackie joined the Kansas City Monarchs as a shortstop. His reputation as an athlete and a man of character made Brooklyn Dodger owner Branch Rickey follow him closely. He was looking for the perfect player to finally end segregation in the Majors. In forty-seven games, Jackie had a .387 average, stole thirteen bases, and was the definition of grace and dignity both on and off the field. Rickey had his man.

In 1946 the experiment was on. Robinson inked a deal to play second base for the Montreal Royals, a Brooklyn farm club. Everyone watched, but especially those in the Negro Leagues, to see how Jackie fared. They knew he could play the keystone corner, but could he hold the keys to their acceptance? In his first game, Robinson went four for five with a home run, four RBI, and two stolen bases. All season he distinguished himself, and the next spring he was called up to the Dodgers. The easy part was over.

His first year in the Majors, Robinson stoically endured incredible abuse. He was called vile, racist names by both spectators and opposing players, and had watermelon chunks hurled at him. This proud competitor was locked in a battle between retaliation and restraint, and knew that to overcome, he had to rise above. It was this wealth of inner strength that made Jackie Robinson just right. A true hero had opened a locked door, then held it open for all those who were counting on him by standing strong, keeping cool, and playing his heart out.

JACKIE ROBINSON

Willie Wells

BORN: AUGUST 10, 1906, AUSTIN, TEXAS
DIED: JANUARY 22, 1989
BATS: RIGHT / THROWS: RIGHT

Elected to the Baseball Hall of Fame in 1997

When Dick Lundy reached the point in his wonderful career to pass on the mantle of "Best Shortstop in Black Baseball," the unanimous choice was the little "Devil," Willie Wells.

The 5'7", 160-pound Texas right-hander wasn't blessed with the greatest arm in the world, but he studied the hitters and played a marvelous "position game." Anticipating where a particular batter would likely hit a certain pitch, Willie was up with the ball quickly and had time to toss his man out. His tremendous ability to go back on popups to left and center fields enabled outfielders to play deep and protect against the extra base hit.

When, in 1936, Wells joined the Newark Eagles, who boasted Ray Dandridge at third, it became nearly impossible to get a hit on the ground through the left side. Awestruck outfielder Monte Irvin described watching Willie "go deep in the hole, get the ball, and flip it to Ray, who would gun the runner at first!" Plays like that got Wells chosen to eight All-Star Games.

Devil carried more than his weight at the plate as well. In his twenty-five-year career from 1923 to 1948, he hit .332 lifetime in the Negro Leagues, with a personal best of .404 in 1930 to win the batting title. He walloped major leaguers for .369 over thirty-one games, with six home runs. After he hit twenty-seven homers in 1927, Willie became a favorite target of pitchers, inventing the batting helmet by wearing a miner's hardhat for protection.

Later, Wells was tapped to become player-manager of the Eagles, and his young charges included Larry Doby and Monte Irvin of future Major League fame. After retiring from baseball, Willie worked in a New York deli before eventually returning to Texas to care for his mother. Wells passed away in the same small house where he was born.

WILLIE WELLS

Charles "Chino" Smith

BORN: 1903, GREENWOOD, SOUTH CAROLINA
DIED: JANUARY 16, 1932
BATS: LEFT / THROWS: RIGHT

Though his time was short, this shooting star from South Carolina left a burning impression on all who caught a glimpse of him. None other than Satchel Paige, who saw them all, swore that Chino Smith was "one of the best *two* hitters in the Negro Leagues."

Chino was a right-handed redcap who played on the Pennsylvania Station team before jumping into pro ball for the Brooklyn Royal Giants. Batting from the left side, he launched line drives to all parts of the park. In 1925 the rookie rapped out a .341 average. By 1927 it had risen to a dizzying .439, but his high mark still lay ahead. In 1929, after a move to the New York Lincoln Giants of the Negro American League, Smith smashed twenty-three home runs, and his average soared to an astronomical .464! On July 5, 1930, in a game against the Brooklyn Black Sox, Chino became the first black man to hit a home run in Yankee Stadium. His strong outfield defense and his spectacular speed on the bases complemented his prowess at the plate. At 5'6" and 168 pounds, this "pocket rocket" was as well rounded a performer as any in the game.

But then, with but seven seasons under his belt, this blazing black ball star fell ill with yellow fever while playing winter ball in Cuba, and at the age of thirty he was gone. At his zenith he had flamed out, leaving fans and fellow pros alike to wonder, amid the fading embers, "What if?"

CHINO SMITH

Andy "Lefty" Cooper

BORN: APRIL 24, 1898, WACO, TEXAS
DIED: JUNE 3, 1941
BATS: RIGHT / THROWS: LEFT

Elected to the Baseball Hall of Fame in 2006

Not all great pitchers win by throwing a 100 mph heater, or a knee-buckling twelve-and-six curve. Some are cuties—hurlers who study the hitters carefully and throw a laundry list of pitches, all at varying speeds to exact locations. With nerves of steel and the guts of a gambler, they employ their accuracy to nibble at the corners of the plate and make befuddled, off-balance batters all but get themselves out. The Kansas City Monarchs's longtime pitcher-manager Andy Cooper was just such a cutie.

The tall Texan broke into baseball with the Detroit Stars in 1920. For the first two seasons he struggled to find his style. But he worked hard, and in doing so honed his command of a great many pitches. Andy sharpened sinkers, sliders, and screwballs by the score. Then, like a hungry marksman with a quiverful of arrows, he went hunting. Over the next six years he went 72-30, and gained the respect of all as one of the keenest minds in baseball.

Andy joined the Kansas City Monarchs in 1928, where he both pitched and managed until 1941. His second year there, he posted a mark of 13-3 and the Monarchs won the Negro National League title. One of Lefty's best years came in 1936 when he went 27-8 against all levels of competition. In 1937 the Negro American League was established and the Monarchs joined as charter members. Cooper steered them to the pennant that year, as well as in 1939, and again in 1940. Tragically, in 1941, at the height of his helmsmanship, Andy fell ill, then suffered a fatal heart attack. He was only forty-five years old.

His life was short, but he was blessed by doing what he loved. Baseball even afforded Cooper his chance to see the world; in the winter of 1933 he joined up with Lonnie Goodwin's Traveling All-Stars for a tour that took him to the Philippines, Japan, and China.

ANDY COOPER

Newt Allen

BORN: MAY 19, 1901, AUSTIN, TEXAS
DIED: JUNE 9, 1988
BATS: RIGHT / THROWS: RIGHT

When the Kansas City Monarchs were formed in 1920, Newt Allen was their ice boy. Two short years later they tried him out at second base, and there the right-hander stayed for the next twenty-two years.

Nicknamed "Colt" for his youthful appearance, Allen was a slick fielder who successfully patterned himself after the great Bingo DeMoss, mastering his famous "no look" throw to first base. In his classy career Newt anchored the infield on eight pennant winners, was elected to four All-Star squads, and often served as team captain. He could play several positions, including third base, where he logged a flawless performance during a 1942 World Series win over the Homestead Grays.

The 5'8", 160-pound switch-hitting Texan was adept with the bat as well. His lifetime average is .296, and he hit a respectable .278 in Cuba. He was considered a skilled bunter and dangerous hit-and-run man. In 1937 the Monarchs joined the new Negro American League, and with Allen at the keystone, they locked up five of the first six pennants.

In one of the young Colt's early outings, he attempted to tag out the rough and seasoned pro Oscar Charleston. As "The Black Ty Cobb" raced like a freight train toward second, Newt fielded the throw nicely and positioned himself for the putout. Charleston had other ideas. Coming in spikes high, Oscar, in Allen's own words, "Cut the glove right off me, and kicked the ball all the way into left field!" Although his hand was forever scarred, the rookie did not rattle. Instead, he absorbed the incident as a valuable baseball lesson, and went on to himself become one of the most daring base runners and slashing sliders the game has ever known.

NEWT ALLEN

Norman "Turkey" Stearnes

BORN: MAY 8, 1901, NASHVILLE, TENNESSEE
DIED: SEPTEMBER 4, 1979
BATS: LEFT / THROWS: LEFT

Elected to the Baseball Hall of Fame in 2000

As far as we know, Turkey Stearnes hit more home runs than any man in black baseball during his era. Although many gaps, or "lost years," appear on the records, all oral accounts assure that the Nashville-born southpaw consistently drove balls out of parks all around the country for over two decades.

After years in the Negro Southern League, Stearnes joined the Detroit Stars in 1923 and announced his arrival with thirty-five home runs. The following year he rang up a personal best of fifty round-trippers. Over the nineteen years that his blasts were being tracked, he won seven home run titles. Turkey perennially posted a batting average in the mid to upper .300s, his best coming in 1935 when he hit .430 to lead the league. The quiet gentleman's lifetime mark is .359, tagged Major Leaguers for .351, and really came alive in postseason play, hitting .474 with four homers in fifteen games.

Satchel Paige once said that as a hitter, "Stearnes was every bit as great" as the more famous Josh Gibson. Turkey never counted his own shots. "If it didn't win a game, it didn't matter," he recalled. "That's all I wanted—for the team to keep on winning." The 160-pound center fielder swung his forty-ounce lumber from an unusual stance. Choking up on the bat, he pointed his right foot at the pitcher and his big toe to heaven, then uncoiled with crushing power. Turkey hit many homers of the 450-500-foot variety. One, in Detroit's Mack Park, traveled 470 feet, and old-timers never forgot the blast that screamed clear out of the St. Louis Stars' cavernous Compton Avenue Park.

Cool Papa Bell put it best, stating, "If they don't put Turkey Stearnes in the Hall of Fame, they shouldn't put anybody in."

TURKEY STEARNES

Jud Wilson

BORN: FEBRUARY 28, 1894, REMINGTON, VIRGINIA
DIED: JUNE 24, 1963
BATS: LEFT / THROWS: RIGHT

Elected to the Baseball Hall of Fame in 2006

Judson Wilson was nicknamed "Boojum" for the cannonlike sound produced by his line drives as they dented outfield fences. Born in Remington, Virginia, in 1894, Wilson became one of the most powerful and consistent hitters in baseball.

Boojum was described as being "built like Hercules" by Hall of Famer Judy Johnson. Outfielder Ted Page added, "He could've gone bear hunting with a switch!" Wilson utilized this great strength to hit screaming liners, and to rack up high averages in an impressive nineteen-year career that ran from 1922 to 1945. Notoriously deadly on low fastballs, Jud earned a reputation as one of the few men who could regularly "wear out" pitching ace Satchel Paige. Jud's .370 lifetime average is the third-highest on the Negro Leagues' all-time list, and his .372 mark in Cuba is their highest ever. Wilson hit over .400 five times in all, and slugged white Major Leaguers for .360. The stubborn lefty crowded the plate on even the hardest throwers, preferring to get hit rather than back off. Wilson smashed his way to six batting crowns. His lone home run title came in Cuba in 1925.

Jud played all around the infield. He wasn't a smooth gloveman, but he hung tough. "More balls hit him in the chest than in the glove," laughed Judy Johnson. Somehow Boojum would make the stop and, once he had the ball, he used his slingshot arm. Wilson's roommate Jake Stephens claimed, "That man could throw out lightning!" The pennant-winning Black Sox of 1929 boasted the finest infield ever assembled, with Oliver Marcelle on third, Dick Lundy at short, Frank Warfield on second, and Wilson at first. Boojum hit .346 that year, and his twenty stolen bases led the league.

JUD WILSON

Louis Santop

BORN: JANUARY 17, 1890, TYLER, TEXAS
DIED: JANUARY 22, 1942
BATS: LEFT / THROWS: RIGHT

Elected to the Baseball Hall of Fame in 2006

Louis Santop played most of his career in the dead-ball era, but that didn't stop "The Top" from blasting some amazing tape-measure home runs. Frank Ford of the New York Lincoln Giants never forgot the day in 1912 when he saw the 6'5", 240-pound catcher smash a shot "five hundred-some feet away! They put up a sign where he hit it." Columnist Red Smith called the big Texan "one of the greatest hitters, black or white, of all time." A ballpark in Newark had a sign 440 feet from home plate offering a free suit to anyone who hit it. When Santop dented it *three times* in one day, they rushed out and took it down. Once, in Atlantic City, he hit a "called shot" home run. A heckler was riding the powerful lefty, predicting a strikeout. Santop bet the woman a buck that he'd drive the ball over the wall in center field, and then did just that. After scoring, he climbed into the stands to collect his winnings. But Louis had more than one way to lose a baseball. Hilldale outfielder Chaney White claimed to have seen him, from a squat behind the plate, "throw a ball *over* the center field fence."

Santop had a lifetime batting average of .303 against black pitching, and hit .316 in games facing white major leaguers. Sadly, Louis's great career ended on a sour note. After batting .376 to lead the Hilldales to the 1924 World Series, Top dropped a two-out pop-up behind the plate in the ninth inning of the deciding game. Given new life, the batter ripped the next pitch for a two-run double, lifting the Kansas City Monarchs to victory. At thirty-four years of age, a dejected Santop decided to hang up his glove.

In retirement, Louis amassed a large collection of Negro League memorabilia, which has since been donated to the Baseball Hall of Fame in Cooperstown.

LOUIS SANTOP

Pete Hill

BORN: OCTOBER 12, 1880, PITTSBURGH, PENNSYLVANIA
DIED: NOVEMBER 26, 1951
BATS: LEFT / THROWS: RIGHT

Elected to the Baseball Hall of Fame in 2006

Preston "Pete" Hill was possibly the craftiest clutch hitter in black ball over the first twenty years of the twentieth century. He was a swift, right-handed center fielder who taught himself to hit lefty, and slashed line drives all over the diamond. With tremendous discipline and the eyes of a hawk, he forced pitchers to throw strikes, and if they did, he rarely missed. It was reported that in 1911 he reached base safely in 115 out of 116 games.

Hill started his career with the Pittsburgh Keystones in 1899, but jumped to the Philadelphia Giants in 1903. He powered them to back-to-back crowns in 1905 and 1906. Along with his potent stick, the bowlegged speed burner brought with him the ability to steal bases at will. Upon reaching first, he faked and feinted starts, and drove opposing pitchers absolutely nuts. His offense, joined with Rube Foster's pitching, made the Giants hard to beat.

Rube convinced Pete and several other stars from Philly and the Leland Giants to form a new club, and by 1910 the spectacular Chicago American Giants were born. They decimated all competition that year going 128-6 with Hill as their captain, and hitting .428 to beat out team-mate Pop Lloyd for the batting title. Foster all but handed the team over to Pete while he busied himself forming the Negro National League, and his confidence was well rewarded. The American Giants won the West crown eleven out of the next twelve years, losing only in 1916 to Oscar Charleston's Indianapolis ABCs.

Pete later moved to the Detroit Stars and continued both in his roles as player-manager, and as one of the most feared hitters in the league. In 1921, he batted cleanup and hit .391 at the age of forty-one. He finished with a lifetime mark of .326, .307 for his six seasons in Cuba, and abused Major League pitching for .354. Once retired, he stayed in Detroit and worked for the Ford Motor Company.

PETE HILL

Ray Brown

BORN: FEBRUARY 23, 1908, ALGER, OHIO
DIED: FEBRUARY 8, 1965
BATS: BOTH / THROWS: RIGHT

Elected to the Baseball Hall of Fame in 2006

The Homestead Grays dynasty of the mid 1930s and 1940s won nine straight pennants with such mighty legends in their lineup as Josh Gibson and Buck Leonard. Yet even the greatest offensive orders cannot be called upon to win ten-run slugfests every day. Students of the game will tell you that while it's nice to get fat at the bat, it's what you do from the mound that gets you crowned. Ray Brown could win that crown.

Ohio-born Brown was a graduate of Wilberforce University. When he joined the Grays, team owner Cumberland Posey picked up more than a star pitcher in the deal, he also signed a son-in-law. He gave the right-hander his daughter's hand in a ceremony at home plate. Posey's new relation went right to work with his sinker, slider, fastball, and terrific curve. Brown went 12-3 in 1935, and over the 1936 and 1937 seasons was the victor in a straight twenty-eight! Ray also played the outfield on his off days, contributing runs to the already potent Grays as a switch-hitter.

Later, Brown added a knuckleball to his arsenal and continued on a tear. The Grays won the pennant in 1940, as Ray went 18-3 and made the All-Star team again. Then, in 1941, he came within a whisker of his previous winning streak by stringing twenty-seven wins. The Grays pocketed another pennant, and bested the New York Cubans for the crown as Brown homered while pitching a shutout in the final game. Like all great competitors, Ray had another gear when it came time for the postseason. In the 1944 Series he one-hit the Birmingham Black Barons. Discontented, he threw a perfect game against the Chicago American Giants the following year.

After leaving the Grays, Brown developed an itchy foot and tossed his spikes and glove over his shoulder to travel around Mexico and Canada for several years, pitching and winning for various clubs into the 1950s.

RAY BROWN

Ted "Double Duty" Radcliffe

BORN: JULY 7, 1902, MOBILE, ALABAMA
DIED: AUGUST 11, 2005
BATS: RIGHT / THROWS: RIGHT

Dubbed "Double Duty" by Damon Runyon, Ted Radcliffe earned the moniker by routinely pitching the first half of a doubleheader, then donning the mask and mitt to catch in the second. But while his duties might have been double, this man from Mobile was surely one of a kind.

A bit of a baseball nomad, "Double Duty" plied his twin trades for over a dozen different teams throughout his twenty-year career. Some were obscure, but some were among the greatest ever assembled. There were no slouches on the pennant-winning 1930 St. Louis Stars, the 1931 Eastern Championship Homestead Grays, or the powerful 1932 Pittsburgh Crawfords, and Ted was on all of those squads. The right-hander posted double-digit wins for each of them, and hit .283, .298, and .325 respectively. Whichever position he played, whether as pitcher who thought like a catcher or a catcher who thought like a pitcher, he was able to bring out the best in his batterymate. He was elected to six All-Star Games, playing three at each position, and the versatile clutch hitter batted .304 in those contests. When, in 1944, Josh Gibson fell ill and began to falter, it was "Double Duty" who was brought back in by the Grays to help carry the load for the legendary backstop.

Pitchers and catchers are a part of every single play, and often set strategy. Athletes from these positions develop a deep understanding of the game, and Radcliffe, having had double exposure, was certainly no exception. It should come as no surprise that after a while Ted was asked to add managing to his already outsized workload.

At the time of his death in 2005, at the grand age of 103, "Double Duty" was the oldest living baseball player.

DOUBLE DUTY RADCLIFFE

Sammy T. Hughes

BORN: OCTOBER 20, 1910, LOUISVILLE, KENTUCKY
DIED: AUGUST 9, 1981
BATS: RIGHT / THROWS: RIGHT

Sammy T. Hughes was the premier second baseman in the Negro Leagues during a sixteen-year career that ran from 1931 to 1946. A defensive player with tremendous range to his right or left, sure leather, and a cannon for an arm, Hughes was a thinking man's infielder, always on top of the situation and rarely making errors. Hall of Famer Cool Papa Bell felt it was a toss-up between Hughes and Bingo DeMoss as to who was the best all-time second baseman in black baseball.

The 6'2", 175-pound right-hander began with the Louisville White Sox, but is best known as the keystone on the oft-moved Elite Giants. Sam played with the Giants in Nashville, Columbus, and Washington, and was still in the lineup when they finally took root in Baltimore. He also played briefly on the powerful Homestead Grays, whose owner, Cumberland Posey, called him a "good hitter, crack fielder, and real baserunner." Hughes leads all Negro Leagues second sackers in East-West All-Star appearances with five, playing three times for the East and twice for the West.

The speedy Hughes was the perfect number two man in the batting order. With fine bat control, he was known for the hit-and-run play, and built up a reputation as a reliable bunter. Hughes batted .277 lifetime in the Black Leagues, and really touched up Major League white pitchers, hitting .353 against them. In 1936 Sam faced one team of white barnstorming All-Stars, led by a young sensation named Bob Feller. Apparently unintimidated, Hughes ripped the future Hall of Fame fastballer for three hits in four at-bats. Sam was so impressive against major leaguers that in the late 1940s, at the tail end of his career, he was still scouted as a prospect for the Pittsburgh Pirates.

SAMMY T. HUGHES

Ray Dandridge

BORN: AUGUST 31, 1913, RICHMOND, VIRGINIA
DIED: FEBRUARY 12, 1994
BATS: RIGHT / THROWS: RIGHT

Elected to the Baseball Hall of Fame in 1987

Nicknamed "Hooks" for his high-performance hands, Ray Dandridge was one of the finest third basemen ever produced by the Negro Leagues. His artistry at the hot corner inspired Hall of Fame outfielder Monte Irvin to declare him "the best third baseman I've ever seen." Ray, who charged everything, would often scoop the ball bare-handed and, without looking, fire a rifle shot over to first to nail the runner. Buck Leonard, in remembering Dandridge, exclaimed, "Anything he got a hand on, *BAM!* You're out!"

The Richmond-born right-hander was no slouch at the plate either. His Negro League lifetime average was .319, and he hit .347 facing white big league pitching. In 1944, as a player-manager for Vera Cruz in the Mexican League, Ray batted .366 and hit in twenty-nine consecutive games to set a league record. That same year, he faced white Major Leaguers five times and, in twenty-two at-bats, hit .455! He was known for his ringing line drives to right field, and his ability to hit behind the runner.

Dandridge was in his mid-thirties, and sixteen years into a twenty-two-year career that stretched from 1933 to 1955, when segregated baseball ended. He was signed by the New York Giants, but sent to their farm club, the Minneapolis Millers. Although he hit .362 and was named 1949 Minor League Rookie of the Year, the Giants decided, based on his age, not to bring Ray up to the Majors for the 1950 season. That decision, said Giants's pitching star Sal "the Barber" Maglie, "cost us the pennant!" Dandridge stayed with the Millers through 1952, playing sparkling ball and providing invaluable advice to the young men just starting out, such as a green centerfielder named Willie Mays, who said, "He was like my dad."

RAY DANDRIDGE

Dick "Cannonball" Redding

BORN: APRIL 14, 1890, ATLANTA, GEORGIA
DIED: OCTOBER 31, 1948
BATS: RIGHT / THROWS: RIGHT

"Cannonball" Redding relied on three basic pitches: hard, hard, and *hard*. The 6'4" Atlanta-born right-hander was purely and simply overpowering. Casey Stengel played against Redding and said, "If he was on a club in the big leagues, he wouldn't lose any games at all!" While Lou Gehrig was still a student at Columbia, the New York Yankees paid Cannonball to pitch to him in an effort to make sure the young first baseman could compete on the Major League level. It has been said the Dick once struck out Babe Ruth three times on nine straight pitches.

Cannonball set the semipro single-game strikeout record by fanning twenty-four in a three-hit gem. In 1912, he won a staggering forty-three games, one of which was a perfect game boasting seventeen strikeouts. Counting semipro outings, he threw twelve no-hitters in his 1911 to 1938 career. Dick started the 1915 season by winning his first twenty games, some against major leaguers. Redding had huge hands and could hide an entire baseball in one palm. Cannonball had an unusual and confusing windup: kicking high with his left leg, he would pivot sharply to face center field, showing the batter his back, then whip back quickly and fire off his heater. Dick was tenacious, and not adverse to pitching inside if a hitter was crowding the plate. He would send that fastball high and tight and, in the words of Judy Johnson, "turn your cap around!"

Cannonball was a superstitious man, and his teammates would chuckle about the way he refused to wash his shirt for weeks at a time during a winning streak, or threw his glove in the garbage after a big loss. But what the men who knew him seem to remember most was that Dick Redding was just a big, happy kid at heart, and that he truly loved life.

CANNONBALL REDDING

Frank Grant

BORN: AUGUST 1, 1865, PITTSFIELD, MASSACHUSETTS
DIED: MAY 27, 1937
BATS: RIGHT / THROWS: RIGHT

Elected to the Baseball Hall of Fame in 2006

When in 1889 the International League chose to adopt the Major League's "color line," it also agreed to kick out its best player, the hard-hitting and fleet-footed defensive marvel, Ulysses Frank Grant.

When he began his pro career, Grant was a pitcher–second baseman in the Eastern League. A short time later he moved up to the International League, a version of today's minor leagues, where he concentrated on second base and began to dominate play. In his first year he hit .344 and sparkled in the field. In his second year, the right-hander hit .353, led in deadball homers with eleven, and stole forty bases for the club in Buffalo, New York, which was a booming city at the time. Comparisons were drawn between him and the finest second baseman in the Majors, Fred Dunlap. Frank was then named the "Best Player in Buffalo History" before being told "get out!" by the league. The door to his dream had been slammed in his face.

After being forced out, the modest man with the soft hands and strong arm moved around some of black baseball's elite early teams. Whether it was for the Cuban Giants, New York Gorhams, Cuban X-Giants, Colored Capital All-Americans, or paired with Home Run Johnson on the Page Fence Giants, Frank distinguished himself with his fine fielding, big bat, and unwavering will to win.

After hanging up his spikes and glove in 1905, Frank moved to New York City, where he quietly lived out his days working as a waiter. He passed away in 1937 from arteriosclerosis but, as those who knew him best would attest, while he had been dealt a bad blow by racism, his great heart had never hardened.

FRANK GRANT

"Bullet" Joe Rogan

BORN: JULY 28, 1889, OKLAHOMA CITY, OKLAHOMA
DIED: MARCH 4, 1967
BATS: RIGHT / THROWS: RIGHT

Elected to the Baseball Hall of Fame in 1998

The nickname "Bullet Joe" conjures images of a power pitcher firing fastball after blazing fastball past hapless hitters. Wilber Rogan was all that and much, much more. The right-handed Bullet was also a master of finesse, possessing a wide variety of sliders, palmballs, changeups, and a nasty jug-handle curve with a three-foot drop. Rogan threw without a windup and fielded his position better than any pitcher in the league. His 109 victories are the second-best record in black ball, yet this is still not the full measure of Bullet Joe.

In his years on the diamond, the Oklahoma-born Bullet held his own at every spot on the team, and played several positions on the same day during doubleheaders. He was a fleet-footed runner who, in 1929 at the age of forty, led the league in stolen bases with twenty-three. But if there was one place where Rogan's talents matched his pitching abilities, it was in the batter's box. Bullet hit clean-up on some of the best teams ever assembled. This 5'9" phenom could shut you down from the mound, then hammer you from the plate with his heavy bat and sweet swing. Rogan pitched and managed the Kansas City Monarchs to three consecutive pennants from 1923 to 1925, while hitting .426, .450, and .355 in those years! His postseason pitching record is 8-4, and he batted .410. His .341 lifetime average is the highest of any pitcher in the Negro Leagues, and he hit major leaguers for .329. Rogan even roughed up the great fireballer Bob Feller's touring All-Stars for three hits—when he was forty-eight years old!

Satchel Paige said of Rogan, "He was one of the world's greatest . . . isn't any maybe so."

BULLET ROGAN

Larry Doby

BORN: DECEMBER 13, 1924, CAMDEN, SOUTH CAROLINA
DIED: JUNE 18, 2003
BATS: LEFT / THROWS: RIGHT

Elected to the Baseball Hall of Fame in 1998

Larry Doby's dad was a ballplayer, and although he passed away when his boy was but eight years old, he had instilled in his son a passion for the game that would take him to the pinnacle of both the Negro and Major Leagues.

Doby graduated from East Side High in Paterson, New Jersey, where he was All-State in baseball, basketball, and football. After attending Long Island University, he joined the Newark Eagles. The right-hander was playing a superb second base, and with a southpaw stick was knocking down the fences when WWII broke out. The only eagle Larry saw for the next few years was on his Navy insignia.

In 1946 Doby returned to Newark and combined forces with Monte Irvin to provide the punch to go with the pitching of Leon Day and Max Manning. It was a powerful team, and the Eagles defeated the Kansas City Monarchs to win the Negro World Series. For the season Larry hit .341, led in triples, and narrowly lost the home run race to Josh Gibson. Doby was peaking at the dawn of a new day.

The following year Jackie Robinson took the field for the Brooklyn Dodgers of the National League and, only four months later, Larry Doby signed with the Cleveland Indians to become the first black man in the American League. In a way, he was Buzz Aldrin to Jackie's Neil Armstrong, having had to suffer all of the hardships with far less of the fanfare because he was "second." Undaunted, Doby shifted to center field, and helped lift Cleveland to the championship in 1948, fulfilling a dream of winning both a Negro League and Major League World Series. He went on to have an All-Star career, finishing tops in power numbers many times. When his days in Cleveland were done, Larry was not. Fond of establishing firsts, he jumped to Japan in 1962 and joined the Chunchi Dragons. Many Major Leaguers now extend their careers in that fashion. Doby's passion never waned, and as late as 1978, he served a stint as manager for the Chicago White Sox.

LARRY DOBY

Elwood "Bingo" DeMoss

BORN: SEPTEMBER 5, 1889, TOPEKA, KANSAS
DIED: JANUARY 26, 1965
BATS: RIGHT / THROWS: RIGHT

Elwood DeMoss mastered the keystone position so brilliantly for more than twenty-five years that an entire generation of black second basemen, those coming of age in the 1930s and 1940s, tried their level best to play "just like Bingo."

DeMoss, who always played with a toothpick in his mouth, was unquestionably the finest defensive second baseman in black ball between the years 1915 and 1925. Many players feel Bingo was the best ever. He was smooth. He had style and grace. He was a "bear down" player who was always "talking it up" to the rest of the infield. His trademark play, which entailed fielding a ground ball and whipping it over to first under his left arm without looking, became the ambition of every young Negro League player. Bingo played on some of the powerhouse Indianapolis ABCs' strongest teams, and was the on-field leader who captained the 1926 Chicago American Giants, considered one of the best ball clubs ever, to a World Series championship.

The much-imitated Kansas-born righty was a solid line-drive hitter who sprayed the ball to all fields. Because of Bingo's excellent bat control, teammate Jelly Gardner remembered, "He wouldn't let you get hung up stealing. If he saw you couldn't make it, he'd get wood on the ball somehow. Foul it off or hit it to right." Bingo hit consistently in the mid to high .200s, and had his best year at the plate in 1926 when he finished second in the batting race with a .303 mark.

When his playing days were over, Bingo DeMoss spent the next fifteen years as a highly respected manager.

BINGO DEMOSS

CF

Alejandro Oms

BORN: MARCH 13, 1895, SANTA CLARA, CUBA
DIED: NOVEMBER 9, 1946
BATS: LEFT / THROWS: LEFT

One of the finest center fielders of the 1920s, Alejandro Oms of Santa Clara, Cuba, was a stylish performer with speed and a sense of showmanship. He covered tremendous ground in the field, and hid a mediocre arm by getting rid of the ball sharply and with absolute accuracy. If the game was not in doubt, he would often entertain the fans with fancy trick catches.

Oms is also regarded as one of the most productive and powerful hitters in the Eastern Colored League's six-year history. From 1923–28 he hit cleanup or higher on the talent-laden Cuban Stars. He excelled on four championship teams, posted perennial batting averages in the mid .300s, and was league leader three times. His personal best slugging percentage was a whopping .619.

Alejandro's flashiness in the field was in direct contrast to his demeanor in the dugout. He actually pretended not to speak English as a way of keeping to himself and opting out of any arguments. But one day, his American teammates rushed to his aid as he lay in the batter's box after being beaned by a pitch. Upon his revival he calmly and clearly requested "a drink of water, please," and his ruse was revealed.

This well-liked Latino lefty finished off his Negro League career with a 2-4 showing in the 1935 East-West All-Star Game. His lifetime average is .332 for his time spent in the States. At home in Cuba, where he was known as "El Caballero" ("The Gentleman"), his lifetime mark is .351 over fifteen years. He was elected to the Cuban Baseball Hall of Fame in 1944.

ALEJANDRO OMS

Dan McClellan

BORN: UNKNOWN
DIED: 1931
BATS: LEFT / THROWS: LEFT

Pitching is, in a way, no different than hitting. People love power. Everyone wants to rear back and rip one off at upward of a hundred miles an hour. Dan McClellan couldn't. It just wasn't there. So instead, in 1903, this southpaw Svengali used his wits with a laundry list of baffling, off-speed breaking stuff to entrance twenty-seven straight batters and send them staggering back to the bench.

It was the first perfect game in black ball history.

Dan pitched his dandy for the Cuban X-Giants, but the very next season he switched to Rube Foster's rotation on the Philadelphia Giants. Together, these two master moundsmen pitched Philly to three consecutive championships. The 1905 Giants were perhaps the greatest team of the shiny new century, with a near-ridiculous record of 134-21-3.

By 1909, McClellan's best pitching days were behind him, but certainly not his playing days. He remained with the Giants, covering center field and batting cleanup. Later, he logged time with the Lincoln Giants and a team called the Smart Set, which in 1912 was involved in a wild affair with the New York Giants. The Giants had agreed to play an exhibition against the Set in New Jersey, but upon arrival were surprised to find the team was black. New York's pitcher, Louis Drucke, refused to take the mound, but 8,000 stomping fans changed his mind. He pulled down the bill of his cap and insisted he be announced as "Pitcher O'Brien." Then, with the game deadlocked in the tenth, the Giants claimed McClellan was using a scuffed, dirty ball. Upon examination, the umpire disagreed and the Giants stormed off, causing a riot. The police swept in as the fans attacked the Giants' fleeing bus.

In 1923, with the Philadelphia Giants of old gone, Dan McClellan pieced together a team by that title and, as player-manager, toured through the Northeast and Canada, marching out a 71-30-3 mark.

DAN McCLELLAN

Burnis "Wild Bill" Wright

BORN: JUNE 6, 1914, MILAN, TENNESSEE
DIED: AUGUST 3, 1996
BATS: BOTH / THROWS: RIGHT

Having dreamt of becoming a pitcher from the age of five, Burnis broke in with his hometown Milan Buffalos in 1931, but quickly earned the nickname "Wild Bill" because of the aerobic training he provided hapless catchers. Even though pitching was obviously not his strong suit, Wright still possessed the stuff for stardom in the Negro Leagues.

After joining the Elite Giants in 1932, Wild Bill became an outstanding outfielder. He also proved to be a sweet-swinging, switch-hitting, clutch cleanup man. He could drag bunt as well as swing for the fences, and was so good that by decade's end he'd been elected to five straight All-Star Games. Wright hit over .400 on two occasions, and finished with a lifetime .361 average. He pounded barnstorming Major Leaguers such as Dizzy Dean and Bob Feller for a mark of .371.

The wild one enjoyed playing his winter ball in Mexico, where he was a fan favorite and consistently led or was near the top of the league in all categories. In 1943, burning it up for the Mexico City Red Devils, Bill had a legendary "monster" year. He was on fire with a .377 first-place batting average, took top honors for RBI with seventy, and his thirteen home runs clipped Roy Campanella by one shot to capture the Triple Crown. Wright's stellar speed was also in evidence as he closed out the season one sack shy of the stolen base title.

Wild Bill so loved Mexico's climate and its people that he moved there and continued playing and coaching until 1956. Upon retiring, he opened an eatery dubbed Bill Wright's Dugout in Aguascalientes, and remained settled south of the border. He was elected to the Mexican Hall of Fame, the Salón de la Fama, in 1982.

BILL WRIGHT

Quincy Trouppe

BORN: DECEMBER 25, 1912, DUBLIN, GEORGIA
DIED: AUGUST 10, 1993
BATS: BOTH / THROWS: RIGHT

Born into the teeming Trouppe troop on Christmas Day 1912, Quincy was the youngest of ten children. Developing a competitive nature was a necessity, as he had to stand up for himself from the start. By the time he was a teenager, Trouppe had become a Golden Gloves boxer, but soon traded in his two sparring mitts for one of the receiver's variety, and shunned throwing hooks in favor of hitting them. In fact, the crafty catcher was one of the great curveball killers in the Negro Leagues.

An alumnus of Missouri's Lincoln College, Quincy started out with the pennant-winning St. Louis Stars in 1931. He later played for both the Kansas City Monarchs and Homestead Grays, and was again a winner with the 1933 Chicago American Giants. After spending the 1938 season with the Indianapolis ABCs, Trouppe traveled to Mexico for several years, where he provided power, defense, and strategy for the Monterrey and Mexico City squads.

The slow-footed, strong-armed switch-hitter carried an above-.300 batting average wherever he went, and always called a smart game.

Trouppe returned to the States in 1944 to assume the mantle of player-manager for the Cleveland Buckeyes, and within a year they were in the Negro World Series against the Grays. Quincy hit .400 as his Buckeyes swept four straight games to claim the crown. The powerful backstop's lifetime average is .311, and he hit .304 for his time in Mexico. He made five East-West All-Star Game appearances, and his side always won.

Trouppe also played in Cuba, Venezuela, Colombia, and Canada. In 1952, at forty years of age, he finally spent a season with the Cleveland Indians of the Major Leagues. After officially hanging up the mask and mitt, Quincy's baseball career came full circle, as he found himself back where the long journey had begun, in St. Louis, this time as a ten-year scout for the Cardinals.

QUINCY TROUPPE

Roy "Campy" Campanella

BORN: NOVEMBER 19, 1921, PHILADELPHIA, PENNSYLVANIA
DIED: JUNE 26, 1993
BATS: RIGHT / THROWS: RIGHT

Elected to the Baseball Hall of Fame in 1969

Roy Campanella had a dream. The teenager desperately wanted to follow in the formidable footsteps of his idol. The high-schooler's hero was the great Negro Leagues' catcher Biz Mackey. Through raw enthusiasm and relentless hard work, the dream became a reality.

After joining the Baltimore Elite Giants in 1937, with the masterful Mackey as his mentor, Campy was on cloud nine. The wide-eyed student absorbed Biz's every whisper, and made a mental note of every mannerism. In 1939, when his teacher transferred to the Newark Eagles, Campy graduated to starter and mimicked Mackey's moves so magnificently, fans were tested to tell that a change had taken place. By 1942, Roy had really come into his own as a catcher, and as a hitter had clubbed his way up to the cleanup spot. Major League teams such as the Pittsburgh Pirates were tracking him, but as of yet were not willing to break the color line.

Campy had a taste for travel as well, and played his winter ball in Cuba, and with Caguas, Santurce, and San Juan in Puerto Rico. He also starred with Monterrey in the Mexican League. But after an impressive five-game exhibition against Major Leaguers in 1945, the burly backstop was Brooklyn bound.

Roy was ready to come straight to the Majors in 1946, but instead spent some time integrating the New England League with the Nashua Dodgers. The Brooklyn farm club immediately won a championship with their new catcher, who was also the league MVP.

Campy got the call to join Jackie Robinson and the big club in 1948, and began a well-documented ten-year Hall of Fame career that featured eight All Star games, three MVPs, five pennants, and a World Series ring.

Tragically, in 1958, the powerful player was paralyzed in an auto accident. Later, during a special event held in his honor, Campy insisted that his old professor of the plate, Biz Mackey, join him on stage for the outpouring of emotional applause.

ROY CAMPANELLA

Stuart "Slim" Jones

BORN: MAY 6, 1913, BALTIMORE, MARYLAND
DIED: DECEMBER 1, 1938
BATS: LEFT / THROWS: LEFT

Due to his long, lean frame, this 6'6", 185-pound, lightning-armed lefty was known as "Slim" Jones when he entered baseball. Soon, his spectacular pitching earned him another moniker—"the southpaw Satchel Paige."

Jones joined his hometown Baltimore Black Sox in 1932, but it was in the Puerto Rican Winter League of 1933 that Slim started firing on all cylinders, striking out 210 men with his low, screaming fastball and whip-crack curve. He returned home gunning for glory, and hit his mark. Jones went 32-4, and his new team, the Philadelphia Stars, swooped into the Championship Series against the Chicago American Giants, where Slim secured the crown with a shutout in the final game.

But the story of 1934 was Slim's outings during two days at Yankee Stadium against his mirror-image rival, Satchel Paige. The first contest was a 10-5 Stars win that many believe included Josh Gibson crushing a Jones fastball out of Yankee Stadium. This unrivaled feat would be a testament to the power of both men. The second tilt would become known as "The Greatest Negro League Game Ever." Over 30,000 fans watched Slim sling a six-inning perfect game to lead Satch's squad 1-0. Oscar Charleston broke it up in the seventh, and the Pittsburgh Crawfords pushed across a run to tie. Slim and Satch dueled mightily, trading strikeouts until the heart-pounding nail-biter was called by nightfall in the tenth.

Jones bested the greatest hitters of his day, yet sadly, he couldn't tame was his own terrible thirst. "Demon Rum" had seized him by the throat, and Slim became a long, unsteady shadow of his former self. In the winter of 1938, the twenty-five-year-old Jones, broke, hocked his overcoat for a bottle of whiskey. As he sank to an alley floor, perhaps he smiled weakly to himself, momentarily mistaking the icy, howling Baltimore wind for the adoring roar of a crowd on some sun-drenched summer field. Before long, he would again be on that glorious field . . . forever.

SLIM JONES

Chet Brewer

BORN: JANUARY 14, 1907, LEAVENWORTH, KANSAS
DIED: MARCH 26, 1990
BATS: BOTH / THROWS: RIGHT

Chet Brewer had a diverse arsenal of deceptive offerings, but they were all such darting devils that disgruntled hitters could draw but one conclusion. When Brewer was pitching, the "doctor" was in.

So clever Chet was at concealing his cuttings, that for over two decades the mischievous moundsman got away with murder. He joined the Kansas City Monarchs in 1924, and within two years, with the help of his hero Bullet Rogan, pitched them to a pennant while posting twenty wins. The Monarchs won again in 1929 as Brewer racked up a 17-3 record, but it was in 1930 that he faced off against Joe Williams of the Homestead Grays in one of the most famous games in Negro Leagues' lore. The forty-five-year-old Smokey Joe decided to beat Brewer at his own game, and the "Battle of the Butchered Balls" was on. For twelve innings the two wizards dueled with dancing orbs of dubious legality. Chet struck out ten straight batters, and nineteen overall, but the Grays' grandmaster fanned twenty-five and pinched the win 1-0!

Brewer toured Asia in 1933, and then pitched twin seasons in Panama, winning a championship. Later he played in the Dominican Republic, throwing a one-hitter against Satchel Paige. Chet threw for Tampico in the Mexican League in 1938, and as the first black American to play south of that border, tossed two no-hitters. The following year he posted twelve wins, but half of them were shutouts. Through much of the 1940s the right-handed rogue toured Latin America and pitched for industrial teams in California.

In 1952, Brewer broke ground as a black manager in the minors for the Southwest International League. Later, he became a long-time instructor and scout for the Pittsburgh Pirates, and was very close friends with Roberto Clemente. Chet was also known for his care of the up-and-coming, and started a youth baseball program in Watts, California, where the local ball field now bears his name.

CHET BREWER

CF

Gene Benson

BORN: OCTOBER 2, 1913, PITTSBURGH, PENNSYLVANIA
DIED: APRIL 5, 1999
BATS: LEFT / THROWS: LEFT

A speedster whose spectacular shoestring snares of sinking line drives were matched for thrill and skill by his equally awesome over-the-shoulder basket catches on deeper blasts, Gene Benson was one well-schooled outfielder. Not surprisingly, his mentor was black baseball's best, Oscar Charleston.

Benson tried out at first base for the Brooklyn Royal Giants in 1932, but they were so high on Highpockets Hudspeth, that Gene switched to the outfield to make the team. He also had to adjust his dream of being a slugger due to some early high strikeout totals. The left-hander persevered by adjusting his stance and becoming a highly effective, Punch and Judy–style, bad-ball hitting, leadoff man.

Bouncing from Brooklyn to the Boston Royals, then to the Bacharachs, it wasn't until 1937 that he found a home to stay with the Philadelphia Stars. Gene slapped around their ace, Slim Jones, so well that Stars' manager Charleston snatched him away from the Bacharachs. It was under his tutelage that Benson became a truly great defensive outfielder.

Gene also enjoyed a long Latin American League career, wintering in Puerto Rico, Cuba, and Mexico. But it was in Venezuela, where as a barnstorming All-Star in 1945 and 1946, that he had a roommate with a destiny—Jackie Robinson. The brown-eyed handsome man had already agreed with Branch Rickey to break the Major League color line next season, but late at night would often wonder, "Why me?" Benson befriended Jackie and reassured the rookie that, "If you can play in the Negro Leagues, you can play *anywhere* . . . you're too smart and too strong to fail!"

Home again, Jackie joined the Majors, and Gene teamed with Satchel Paige's All-Stars to tour the States, playing an All-Star team belonging to Bob Feller, whom Benson hit well. By 1949 Gene's young friend was a big star with the Dodgers, but his own playing days were done. He stayed in Philly, the city he loved, worked for the school district, and played his violin.

GENE BENSON

James "Cool Papa" Bell

BORN: MAY 17, 1903, STARKVILLE, MISSISSIPPI
DIED: MARCH 7, 1991
BATS: BOTH / THROWS: LEFT

Elected to the Baseball Hall of Fame in 1974

"Cool was *so* fast, he could switch off the light and be in bed before the room got dark!" said Satchel Paige—and in all likelihood, James "Cool Papa" Bell was the fastest man ever to play baseball. Whether lashing across the outfield to snare a line drive in the gap, or blazing a trail around the bases, for twenty-six years Bell gave fans a run for their money, and they loved every minute.

Cool Papa started his career in 1922 as a pitcher, but it was soon obvious that a man with his speed belonged on the basepaths on a daily basis. Cool playing every day meant good attendance every day, too; people crowded in to see him do the astounding, such as scoring from second on a routine fly ball, or even from first on a sacrifice. In the 1933 season, Bell stole 175 basses. Legend has it he even swiped two of them on a single pitch! Timed by stopwatch, he ran the bases in twelve seconds flat and, understandably, the "inside the park" homer was his specialty. During the 1934 All-Star Game, he scored the game-winning run by scorching all the way from second on a ground ball.

Bell compiled a .339 lifetime batting average in the Negro Leagues, and in fifty-four outings against white Major Leaguers, he hit .392. Playing in Mexico in 1940, he hit .437 and led the league in every category, including homers. In 1946, at the age of forty-three, Cool Papa was hitting .411 and locked in a race for the batting title with Monte Irvin. Bell purposely sat out the season's last two games and gave the crown to Irvin because, in his words, "For the first time the Major Leagues were serious about taking in blacks. I was too old, but Monte was young and had a chance for a future. It was important he be noticed, important that he get that chance." Cool, Papa.

COOL PAPA BELL

*To my big brother Paul, who can still snap off a wicked curve after all these years,
and to my big brother Robert, who launched my love of the Yankees way back in the
dismal days of Horace Clarke and Danny Cater.* —M. C.

*To my twins, Tony and Tessa, in the hopes that they one day
find a friend like Mark.* —J. M.

ACKNOWLEDGMENTS

A special thanks to James Riley, Monte Irvin, Matt Goebel, Todd Bolton, Phil Dixon,
John Holway, Larry Hogan, Dick Clark, Jenette Kahn, John Van Fleet,
Mike and Christine Mignola, Paul Curtis, and, of course, Charlie Kochman.

EDITOR: Charles Kochman
DESIGNER: Brady McNamara
PRODUCTION MANAGER: Jules Thomson

LIBRARY OF CONGRESS CATALOGING-IN-PUBLICATION DATA
Morelli, Jack.
   Heroes of the Negro leagues / by Jack Morelli ;
   illustrated by Mark Chiarello.
     p. cm.
   ISBN 13: 978-0-8109-9434-8 (hardcover with jacket)
   ISBN 10: 0-8109-9434-8 (hardcover with jacket)
   1. Negro leagues—History—Juvenile literature.
   2. African American baseball players—Biography.
   3. Baseball—United States—History. I. Title.

   GV863.A1M63 2007
   796.3570922—dc22
   [B]   2007007391

PUBLISHED IN 2007 BY ABRAMS,
AN IMPRINT OF HARRY N. ABRAMS, INC.

Printed and bound in China
10 9 8 7 6 5 4 3 2 1

HNA

harry n. abrams, inc.
a subsidiary of La Martinière Groupe

115 West 18th Street
New York, NY 10011
www.hnabooks.com